THE GLASS MENAGERIE

Tennessee Williams

SPARK PUBLISHING

Spark Publishing
A Division of Barnes & Noble
120 Fifth Avenue
New York, NY 10011
www.sparknotes.com

ISBN-13: 978-1-4114-0734-3
ISBN-10: 1-4114-0734-2

Please submit changes or report errors to www.sparknotes.com/errors.

Printed in the United States.

10 9 8 7 6 5 4 3 2 1

CONTENTS

CONTEXT

TENNESSEE WILLIAMS WAS BORN in Columbus, Mississippi, in 1911. The name given to him at birth was Thomas Lanier Williams III. He did not acquire the nickname Tennessee until college, when classmates began calling him that in honor of his Southern accent and his father's home state. The Williams family had produced several illustrious politicians in the state of Tennessee, but Williams's grandfather had squandered the family fortune. Williams's father, C.C. Williams, was a traveling salesman and a heavy drinker. Williams's mother, Edwina, was a Mississippi clergyman's daughter and prone to hysterical attacks. Until Williams was seven, he, his parents, his older sister, Rose, and his younger brother, Dakin, lived with Edwina's parents in Mississippi. After that, the family moved to St. Louis. Once there, the family's situation deteriorated. C.C.'s drinking increased, the family moved sixteen times in ten years, and the young Williams, always shy and fragile, was ostracized and taunted at school. During these years, he and Rose became extremely close. Rose, the model for Laura in *The Glass Menagerie,* suffered from mental illness later in life and eventually underwent a prefrontal lobotomy (an intensive brain surgery), an event that was extremely upsetting for Williams.

An average student and social outcast in high school, Williams turned to the movies and writing for solace. At sixteen, Williams won five dollars in a national competition for his answer to the question "Can a good wife be a good sport?"; his answer was published in *Smart Set* magazine. The next year, he published a horror story in a magazine called *Weird Tales,* and the year after that he entered the University of Missouri as a journalism major. While there, he wrote his first plays. Before Williams could receive his degree, however, his father, outraged because Williams had failed a required ROTC program course, forced him to withdraw from school and go to work at the same shoe company where he himself worked.

Williams worked at the shoe factory for three years, a job that culminated in a minor nervous breakdown. After that, he returned to college, this time at Washington University in St. Louis. While he was studying there, a St. Louis theater group produced his plays *The Fugitive Kind* and *Candles to the Sun.* Personal problems led

Williams to drop out of Washington University and enroll in the University of Iowa. While he was in Iowa, his sister, Rose, underwent a lobotomy, which left her institutionalized for the rest of her life. Despite this trauma, Williams finally graduated in 1938. In the years that followed, he lived a bohemian life, working menial jobs and wandering from city to city. He continued to work on drama, however, receiving a Rockefeller grant and studying playwriting at the New School in New York. During the early years of World War II, Williams worked in Hollywood as a scriptwriter.

Around 1941, Williams began the work that would become *The Glass Menagerie*. The play evolved from a short story entitled "Portrait of a Girl in Glass," which focused more completely on Laura than the play does. In December of 1944, *The Glass Menagerie* was staged in Chicago, with the collaboration of a number of well-known theatrical figures. When the play first opened, the audience was sparse, but the Chicago critics raved about it, and eventually it was playing to full houses. In March of 1945, the play moved to Broadway, where it won the prestigious New York Drama Critics' Circle Award. This highly personal, explicitly autobiographical play earned Williams fame, fortune, and critical respect, and it marked the beginning of a successful run that would last for another ten years. Two years after *The Glass Menagerie*, Williams won another Drama Critics' Circle Award and a Pulitzer Prize for *A Streetcar Named Desire*. Williams won the same two prizes again in 1955, for *Cat on a Hot Tin Roof*.

The impact of success on Williams's life was colossal and, in his estimation, far from positive. In an essay entitled "The Catastrophe of Success," he outlines, with both light humor and a heavy sense of loss, the dangers that fame poses for an artist. For years after he became a household name, Williams continued to mine his own experiences to create pathos-laden works. Alcoholism, depression, thwarted desire, loneliness in search of purpose, and insanity were all part of Williams's world. Since the early 1940s, he had been a known homosexual, and his experiences in an era and culture unfriendly to homosexuality certainly affected his work. After 1955, Williams began using drugs, and he would later refer to the 1960s as his "stoned age." He suffered a period of intense depression after the death of his longtime partner in 1961 and, six years later, entered a psychiatric hospital in St. Louis. He continued to write nonetheless, though most critics agree that the quality of his work diminished in his later life. His life's work adds up to twenty-five full-length plays, five screenplays, over seventy one-act plays, hundreds of short stories, two novels, poetry, and a memoir; five of his plays were also made into movies. Williams died from choking in a drug-related incident in 1983.

THE GLASS MENAGERIE IN PERFORMANCE

When *The Glass Menagerie* was first produced in Chicago in 1944, Tennessee Williams was an obscure, struggling playwright. He had recently quit a job in Los Angeles writing screenplays for MGM, an experience he had not considered positive. An adaptation he had been assigned to do for the famous actress Lana Turner was rejected as unsuitable for her; Williams described Turner in his *Memoirs* as unable to "act her way out of her form-fitting cashmere."

Thanks to the efforts of Williams's faithful agent, Audrey Wood, *The Glass Menagerie* was picked up by Eddie Dowling, an actor, director, and producer. Dowling grabbed the role of Tom for himself and persuaded Laurette Taylor to take on the role of Amanda. Taylor, who had become a darling of the American stage for her performance as the title character in *Peg o' My Heart* in 1912, had been living in semi-reclusion since the death of her husband in 1928. Bringing her into *The Glass Menagerie* was both a great coup and a substantial gamble. A shadowy Chicago entrepreneur whose main business was running seedy hotels financed the production. Legend has it that the rehearsals for the play did not inspire optimism; for one thing, Taylor seemed in constant danger of forgetting her lines.

Opening night was December 26, 1944. Not long before the curtain rose, the cast and crew panicked when they could not find Ms. Taylor. She was quickly discovered, however, in the bathroom, attempting to put on a bathrobe that she was to wear later in the play. Taylor, along with the other cast members, went on to give a magnificent performance. The next day, newspaper critics raved about the play and its cast. Oddly, though, attendance was sparse for the remainder of the first week. The financial backer was on the verge of closing the play, but Chicago's theater critics mounted an all-out campaign to save it, begging readers of their daily columns not to miss the play. Within another couple of weeks, *The Glass Menagerie* was playing to full houses.

In March of 1945, the play opened at the Playhouse Theatre in New York. The cast was the same one that had played in Chicago, with Julie Haydon as Laura and Anthony Ross as Jim. The play's reception in New York was every bit as strong as in Chicago. It ran for 561 performances and was named best American play of the year by the New York Drama Critics' Circle.

Laurette Taylor's performance as Amanda went on to become the stuff of myth. When *The Glass Menagerie* was revived on Broadway in 1956, Helen Hayes's interpretation of the role was judged as acceptable but lacking Taylor's magic. Maureen Stapleton met the same fate playing Amanda on Broadway in 1965. In 1973, the American Broadcasting Corporation staged *The Glass Menagerie* for television, with Katherine Hepburn as Amanda. Hepburn's performance was praised to the skies, as was the production as a whole, with Sam Waterston as Tom, Joanna Miles as Laura, and Michael Moriarty as Jim (Moriarty's performance was said to mark a watershed in the interpretation of Jim's character).

The success of the ABC production points to an important aspect of the play: the cinematic quality of its staging. Its use of music to enhance atmosphere and drama is reminiscent of film technique, and its use of lighting to emphasize a character's reaction or to show his or her face in a new light resembles the way in which movies use close-up shots to create the same effects. Even the words that appear on the screen have something in common with the titles of silent films. Nonetheless, the two film versions of the play were relatively lackluster. A 1950 film version, directed by Irving Rapper and starring Gertrude Lawrence as Amanda, manufactured a happier ending for the story; critics and Williams himself hated it. In 1987, Paul Newman directed a talented cast (John Malkovich as Tom, Joanne Woodward as Amanda, Karen Allen as Laura) in another film version, which met with reviews that ranged from lukewarm to hostile.

Almost all performances of *The Glass Menagerie* have followed the Acting Edition of the play, created to reflect the dialogue and staging of the first production. The Acting Edition varies a fair bit from the Reading Edition, which is the version that is anthologized in collections of Williams's works and the version he preferred to hand down to posterity. The Acting Edition calls for more realistic lighting and over 1,000 minor changes in the dialogue. Its most significant difference from the Reading Edition, however, is its elimination of the screen on which words and images are periodically projected. Eddie Dowling, the director of the first production, found the screen device awkward, and subsequent directors have largely concurred, calling it pretentious and condescending, choosing to stage the play without it. In general, staged productions of the play tend to downplay its expressionist, symbolic, and blatantly nonrealistic elements, opting instead for a more realistic, natural interpretation of Williams's dialogue. One of the few productions to follow the Reading Edition, leaving the screen intact, was directed by the theater critic Geoffrey Borny in Australia.

Plot Overview

THE GLASS MENAGERIE is a *memory play*, and its action is drawn from the memories of the narrator, Tom Wingfield. Tom is a character in the play, which is set in St. Louis in 1937. He is an aspiring poet who toils in a shoe warehouse to support his mother, Amanda, and sister, Laura. Mr. Wingfield, Tom and Laura's father, ran off years ago and, except for one postcard, has not been heard from since.

Amanda, originally from a genteel Southern family, regales her children frequently with tales of her idyllic youth and the scores of suitors who once pursued her. She is disappointed that Laura, who wears a brace on her leg and is painfully shy, does not attract any gentlemen callers. She enrolls Laura in a business college, hoping that she will make her own and the family's fortune through a business career. Weeks later, however, Amanda discovers that Laura's crippling shyness has led her to drop out of the class secretly and spend her days wandering the city alone. Amanda then decides that Laura's last hope must lie in marriage and begins selling magazine subscriptions to earn the extra money she believes will help to attract suitors for Laura. Meanwhile, Tom, who loathes his warehouse job, finds escape in liquor, movies, and literature, much to his mother's chagrin. During one of the frequent arguments between mother and son, Tom accidentally breaks several of the glass animal figurines that are Laura's most prized possessions.

Amanda and Tom discuss Laura's prospects, and Amanda asks Tom to keep an eye out for potential suitors at the warehouse. Tom selects Jim O'Connor, a casual friend, and invites him to dinner. Amanda quizzes Tom about Jim and is delighted to learn that he is a driven young man with his mind set on career advancement. She prepares an elaborate dinner and insists that Laura wear a new dress. At the last minute, Laura learns the name of her caller; as it turns out, she had a devastating crush on Jim in high school. When Jim arrives, Laura answers the door, on Amanda's orders, and then quickly disappears, leaving Tom and Jim alone. Tom confides to Jim that he has used the money for his family's electric bill to join the merchant marine and plans to leave his job and family in search of adventure. Laura refuses to eat dinner with the others, feigning

7

illness. Amanda, wearing an ostentatious dress from her glamorous youth, talks vivaciously with Jim throughout the meal.

As dinner is ending, the lights go out as a consequence of the unpaid electric bill. The characters light candles, and Amanda encourages Jim to entertain Laura in the living room while she and Tom clean up. Laura is at first paralyzed by Jim's presence, but his warm and open behavior soon draws her out of her shell. She confesses that she knew and liked him in high school but was too shy to approach him. They continue talking, and Laura reminds him of the nickname he had given her: "Blue Roses," an accidental corruption of pleurosis, an illness Laura had in high school. He reproaches her for her shyness and low self-esteem but praises her uniqueness. Laura then ventures to show him her favorite glass animal, a unicorn. Jim dances with her, but in the process, he accidentally knocks over the unicorn, breaking off its horn. Laura is forgiving, noting that now the unicorn is a normal horse. Jim then kisses her, but he quickly draws back and apologizes, explaining that he was carried away by the moment and that he actually has a serious girlfriend. Resigned, Laura offers him the broken unicorn as a souvenir.

Amanda enters the living room, full of good cheer. Jim hastily explains that he must leave because of an appointment with his fiancée. Amanda sees him off warmly but, after he is gone, turns on Tom, who had not known that Jim was engaged. Amanda accuses Tom of being an inattentive, selfish dreamer and then throws herself into comforting Laura. From the fire escape outside of their apartment, Tom watches the two women and explains that, not long after Jim's visit, he gets fired from his job and leaves Amanda and Laura behind. Years later, though he travels far, he finds that he is unable to leave behind guilty memories of Laura.

CHARACTER LIST

Amanda Wingfield Laura and Tom's mother. A proud, vivacious woman, Amanda clings fervently to memories of a vanished, genteel past. She is simultaneously admirable, charming, pitiable, and laughable.

Laura Wingfield Amanda's daughter and Tom's older sister. Laura has a bad leg, on which she has to wear a brace, and walks with a limp. Twenty-three years old and painfully shy, she has largely withdrawn from the outside world and devotes herself to old records and her collection of glass figurines.

Tom Wingfield Amanda's son and Laura's younger brother. An aspiring poet, Tom works at a shoe warehouse to support the family. He is frustrated by the numbing routine of his job and escapes from it through movies, literature, and alcohol.

Jim O'Connor An old acquaintance of Tom and Laura. Jim was a popular athlete in high school and is now a shipping clerk at the shoe warehouse in which Tom works. He is unwaveringly devoted to goals of professional achievement and ideals of personal success.

Mr. Wingfield Amanda's husband and Laura and Tom's father. Mr. Wingfield was a handsome man who worked for a telephone company. He abandoned his family years before the action of the play and never appears onstage. His picture, however, is prominently displayed in the Wingfields' living room.

ANALYSIS OF MAJOR CHARACTERS

TOM WINGFIELD

Tom's double role in *The Glass Menagerie*—as a character whose recollections the play documents and as a character who acts within those recollections—underlines the play's tension between objectively presented dramatic truth and memory's distortion of truth. Unlike the other characters, Tom sometimes addresses the audience directly, seeking to provide a more detached explanation and assessment of what has been happening onstage. But at the same time, he demonstrates real and sometimes juvenile emotions as he takes part in the play's action. This duality can frustrate our understanding of Tom, as it is hard to decide whether he is a character whose assessments should be trusted or one who allows his emotions to affect his judgment. It also shows how the nature of recollection is itself problematic: memory often involves confronting a past in which one was less virtuous than one is now. Because *The Glass Menagerie* is partly autobiographical, and because Tom is a stand-in for the playwright himself (Williams's given name was Thomas, and he, like Tom, spent part of his youth in St. Louis with an unstable mother and sister, his father absent much of the time), we can apply this comment on the nature of memory to Williams's memories of his own youth.

Even taken as a single character, Tom is full of contradiction. On the one hand, he reads literature, writes poetry, and dreams of escape, adventure, and higher things. On the other hand, he seems inextricably bound to the squalid, petty world of the Wingfield household. We know that he reads D. H. Lawrence and follows political developments in Europe, but the content of his intellectual life is otherwise hard to discern. We have no idea of Tom's opinion on Lawrence, nor do we have any indication of what Tom's poetry is about. All we learn is what he thinks about his mother, his sister, and his warehouse job—precisely the things from which he claims he wants to escape.

Tom's attitude toward Amanda and Laura has puzzled critics. Even though he clearly cares for them, he is frequently indifferent and even cruel toward them. His speech at the close of the play demonstrates his strong feelings for Laura. But he cruelly deserts her and Amanda, and not once in the course of the play does he behave kindly or lovingly toward Laura—not even when he knocks down her glass menagerie. Critics have suggested that Tom's confusing behavior indicates an incestuous attraction toward his sister and his shame over that attraction. This theory casts an interesting light on certain moments of the play—for example, when Amanda and Tom discuss Laura at the end of Scene Five. Tom's insistence that Laura is hopelessly peculiar and cannot survive in the outside world, while Amanda (and later Jim) claims that Laura's oddness is a positive thing, could have as much to do with his jealous desire to keep his sister to himself as with Laura's own quirks.

Amanda Wingfield

If there is a signature character type that marks Tennessee Williams's dramatic work, it is undeniably that of the faded Southern belle. Amanda is a clear representative of this type. In general, a Tennessee Williams faded belle is from a prominent Southern family, has received a traditional upbringing, and has suffered a reversal of economic and social fortune at some point in her life. Like Amanda, these women all have a hard time coming to terms with their new status in society—and indeed, with modern society in general, which disregards the social distinctions that they were taught to value. Their relationships with men and their families are turbulent, and they staunchly defend the values of their past. As with Amanda, their maintenance of genteel manners in very ungenteel surroundings can appear tragic, comic, or downright grotesque. Amanda is the play's most extroverted and theatrical character, and one of modern American drama's most coveted female roles (the acclaimed stage actress Laurette Taylor came out of semi-retirement to play the role in the original production, and a number of legendary actresses, including Jessica Tandy, have since taken on the role).

Amanda's constant nagging of Tom and her refusal to see Laura for who she really is are certainly reprehensible, but Amanda also reveals a willingness to sacrifice for her loved ones that is in many ways unparalleled in the play. She subjects herself to the humiliating drudgery of subscription sales in order to enhance Laura's marriage prospects, without ever uttering so much as a word of complaint. The safest conclusion to draw is that Amanda is not evil but is deeply flawed. In fact, her flaws are centrally responsible for the tragedy, comedy, and theatrical flair of her character. Like her children, Amanda withdraws from reality into fantasy. Unlike them, she is convinced that she is not doing so and, consequently, is constantly making efforts to engage with people and the world outside her family. Amanda's monologues to her children, on the phone, and to Jim all reflect quite clearly her moral and psychological failings, but they are also some of the most colorful and unforgettable words in the play.

Laura Wingfield

The physically and emotionally crippled Laura is the only character in the play who never does anything to hurt anyone else. Despite the weight of her own problems, she displays a pure compassion— as with the tears she sheds over Tom's unhappiness, described by Amanda in Scene Four—that stands in stark contrast to the selfishness and grudging sacrifices that characterize the Wingfield household. Laura also has the fewest lines in the play, which contributes to her aura of selflessness. Yet she is the axis around which the plot turns, and the most prominent symbols—blue roses, the glass unicorn, the entire glass menagerie—all in some sense represent her. Laura is as rare and peculiar as a blue rose or a unicorn, and she is as delicate as a glass figurine.

Other characters seem to assume that, like a piece of transparent glass, which is colorless until light shines upon it, Laura can take on whatever color they wish. Thus, Amanda both uses the contrast between herself and Laura to emphasize the glamour of her own youth and to fuel her hope of re-creating that youth through Laura. Tom and Jim both see Laura as an exotic creature, completely and rather quaintly foreign to the rest of the world. Yet Laura's crush on the high school hero, Jim, is a rather ordinary schoolgirl sentiment, and a girl as supposedly fragile as Laura could hardly handle the days she spends walking the streets in the cold to avoid going to typing class. Through actions like these, Laura repeatedly displays a will of her own that defies others' perceptions of her, and this will repeatedly goes unacknowledged.

Themes, Motifs & Symbols

Themes

Themes are the fundamental and often universal ideas explored in a literary work.

The Difficulty of Accepting Reality

Among the most prominent and urgent themes of *The Glass Menagerie* is the difficulty the characters have in accepting and relating to reality. Each member of the Wingfield family is unable to overcome this difficulty, and each, as a result, withdraws into a private world of illusion where he or she finds the comfort and meaning that the real world does not seem to offer. Of the three Wingfields, reality has by far the weakest grasp on Laura. The private world in which she lives is populated by glass animals—objects that, like Laura's inner life, are incredibly fanciful and dangerously delicate. Unlike his sister, Tom is capable of functioning in the real world, as we see in his holding down a job and talking to strangers. But, in the end, he has no more motivation than Laura does to pursue professional success, romantic relationships, or even ordinary friendships, and he prefers to retreat into the fantasies provided by literature and movies and the stupor provided by drunkenness. Amanda's relationship to reality is the most complicated in the play. Unlike her children, she is partial to real-world values and longs for social and financial success. Yet her attachment to these values is exactly what prevents her from perceiving a number of truths about her life. She cannot accept that she is or should be anything other than the pampered belle she was brought up to be, that Laura is peculiar, that Tom is not a budding businessman, and that she herself might be in some ways responsible for the sorrows and flaws of her children. Amanda's retreat into illusion is in many ways more pathetic than her children's, because it is not a willful imaginative construction but a wistful distortion of reality.

Although the Wingfields are distinguished and bound together by the weak relationships they maintain with reality, the illusions to which they succumb are not merely familial quirks. The outside world is just as susceptible to illusion as the Wingfields. The young people at the Paradise Dance Hall waltz under the short-lived illusion created by a glass ball—another version of Laura's glass animals. Tom opines to Jim that the other viewers at the movies he attends are substituting on-screen adventure for real-life adventure, finding fulfillment in illusion rather than real life. Even Jim, who represents the "world of reality," is banking his future on public speaking and the television and radio industries—all of which are means for the creation of illusions and the persuasion of others that these illusions are true. *The Glass Menagerie* identifies the conquest of reality by illusion as a huge and growing aspect of the human condition in its time.

THE IMPOSSIBILITY OF TRUE ESCAPE

At the beginning of Scene Four, Tom regales Laura with an account of a magic show in which the magician managed to escape from a nailed-up coffin. Clearly, Tom views his life with his family and at the warehouse as a kind of coffin—cramped, suffocating, and morbid—in which he is unfairly confined. The promise of escape, represented by Tom's missing father, the Merchant Marine Service, and the fire escape outside the apartment, haunts Tom from the beginning of the play, and in the end, he does choose to free himself from the confinement of his life.

The play takes an ambiguous attitude toward the moral implications and even the effectiveness of Tom's escape. As an able-bodied young man, he is locked into his life not by exterior factors but by emotional ones—by his loyalty to and possibly even love for Laura and Amanda. Escape for Tom means the suppression and denial of these emotions in himself, and it means doing great harm to his mother and sister. The magician is able to emerge from his coffin without upsetting a single nail, but the human nails that bind Tom to his home will certainly be upset by his departure. One cannot say for certain that leaving home even means true escape for Tom. As far as he might wander from home, something still "pursue[s]" him. Like a jailbreak, Tom's escape leads him not to freedom but to the life of a fugitive.

THE UNRELENTING POWER OF MEMORY

According to Tom, *The Glass Menagerie* is a memory play—both its style and its content are shaped and inspired by memory. As Tom himself states clearly, the play's lack of realism, its high drama, its overblown and too-perfect symbolism, and even its frequent use of music are all due to its origins in memory. Most fictional works are products of the imagination that must convince their audience that they are something else by being realistic. A play drawn from memory, however, is a product of real experience and hence does not need to drape itself in the conventions of realism in order to seem real. The creator can cloak his or her true story in unlimited layers of melodrama and unlikely metaphor while still remaining confident of its substance and reality. Tom—and Tennessee Williams—take full advantage of this privilege.

The story that the play tells is told because of the inflexible grip it has on the narrator's memory. Thus, the fact that the play exists at all is a testament to the power that memory can exert on people's lives and consciousness. Indeed, Williams writes in the Production Notes that "nostalgia . . . is the first condition of the play." The narrator, Tom, is not the only character haunted by his memories. Amanda too lives in constant pursuit of her bygone youth, and old records from her childhood are almost as important to Laura as her glass animals. For these characters, memory is a crippling force that prevents them from finding happiness in the present or the offerings of the future. But it is also the vital force for Tom, prompting him to the act of creation that culminates in the achievement of the play.

MOTIFS

Motifs are recurring structures, contrasts, and literary devices that can help to develop and inform the text's major themes.

ABANDONMENT
The plot of *The Glass Menagerie* is structured around a series of abandonments. Mr. Wingfield's desertion of his family determines their life situation; Jim's desertion of Laura is the center of the play's dramatic action; Tom's abandonment of his family gives him the distance that allows him to shape their story into a narrative. Each of these acts of desertion proves devastating for those left behind. At the same time, each of them is portrayed as the necessary condition for, and a natural result of, inevitable progress. In particular, each is strongly associated with the march of technological progress and the achievements of the modern world. Mr. Wingfield, who works for the telephone company, leaves his family because he "fell in love with [the] long distances" that the telephone brings into people's consciousness. It is impossible to imagine that Jim, who puts his faith in the future of radio and television, would tie himself to the

sealed, static world of Laura. Tom sees his departure as essential to the pursuit of "adventure," his taste for which is whetted by the movies he attends nightly. Only Amanda and Laura, who are devoted to archaic values and old memories, will presumably never assume the role of abandoner and are doomed to be repeatedly abandoned.

THE WORDS AND IMAGES ON THE SCREEN

One of the play's most unique stylistic features is the use of an onstage screen on which words and images relevant to the action are projected. Sometimes the screen is used to emphasize the importance of something referred to by the characters, as when an image of blue roses appears in Scene Two; sometimes it refers to something from a character's past or fantasy, as when the image of Amanda as a young girl appears in Scene Six. At other times, it seems to function as a slate for impersonal commentary on the events and characters of the play, as when "Ou sont les neiges" (words from a fifteenth-century French poem praising beautiful women) appear in Scene One as Amanda's voice is heard offstage.

What appears on the screen generally emphasizes themes or symbols that are already established quite obviously by the action of the play. The device thus seems at best ironic, and at worst somewhat pretentious or condescending. Directors who have staged the play have been, for the most part, very ambivalent about the effectiveness and value of the screen, and virtually all have chosen to eliminate it from the performance. The screen is, however, an interesting epitome of Tennessee Williams's expressionist theatrical style, which downplays realistic portrayals of life in favor of stylized presentations of inner experience.

MUSIC

Music is used often in *The Glass Menagerie,* both to emphasize themes and to enhance the drama. Sometimes the music is extra-diegetic—coming from outside the play, not from within it—and though the audience can hear it the characters cannot. For example, a musical piece entitled "The Glass Menagerie," written specifically for the play by the composer Paul Bowles, plays when Laura's character or her glass collection comes to the forefront of the action. This piece makes its first appearance at the end of Scene One, when Laura notes that Amanda is afraid that her daughter will end up an old maid. Other times, the music comes from inside the diegetic space of the play—that is, it is a part of the action, and the characters can hear it. Examples of this are the music that wafts up from the Paradise Dance Hall and the music Laura plays on her record player. Both the extra-diegetic and the diegetic music often provide commentary on what is going on in the play. For example, the Paradise Dance Hall plays a piece entitled "The World Is Waiting for the Sunrise" while Tom is talking about the approach of World War II.

SYMBOLS

Symbols are objects, characters, figures, and colors used to represent abstract ideas or concepts.

LAURA'S GLASS MENAGERIE

As the title of the play informs us, the glass menagerie, or collection of animals, is the play's central symbol. Laura's collection of glass animal figurines represents a number of facets of her personality. Like the figurines, Laura is delicate, fanciful, and somehow old-fashioned. Glass is transparent, but, when light is shined upon it correctly, it refracts an entire rainbow of colors. Similarly, Laura, though quiet and bland around strangers, is a source of strange, multifaceted delight to those who choose to look at her in the right light. The menagerie also represents the imaginative world to which Laura devotes herself—a world that is colorful and enticing but based on fragile illusions.

THE GLASS UNICORN

The glass unicorn in Laura's collection—significantly, her favorite figure—represents her peculiarity. As Jim points out, unicorns are "extinct" in modern times and are lonesome as a result of being different from other horses. Laura too is unusual, lonely, and ill-adapted to existence in the world in which she lives. The fate of the unicorn is also a smaller-scale version of Laura's fate in Scene Seven. When Jim dances with and then kisses Laura, the unicorn's horn breaks off, and it becomes just another horse. Jim's advances endow Laura with a new normalcy, making her seem more like just another girl, but the violence with which this normalcy is thrust upon her means that Laura cannot become normal without somehow shattering. Eventually, Laura gives Jim the unicorn as a "souvenir." Without its horn, the unicorn is more appropriate for him than for her, and the broken figurine represents all that he has taken from her and destroyed in her.

"BLUE ROSES"

Like the glass unicorn, "Blue Roses," Jim's high school nickname for Laura, symbolizes Laura's unusualness yet allure. The name is also associated with Laura's attraction to Jim and the joy that his kind treatment brings her. Furthermore, it recalls Tennessee Williams's sister, Rose, on whom the character of Laura is based.

THE FIRE ESCAPE

Leading out of the Wingfields' apartment is a fire escape with a landing. The fire escape represents exactly what its name implies: an escape from the fires of frustration and dysfunction that rage in the Wingfield household. Laura slips on the fire escape in Scene Four, highlighting her inability to escape from her situation. Tom, on the other hand, frequently steps out onto the landing to smoke, anticipating his eventual getaway.

Summary & Analysis

Scenes One & Two

Summary: Scene One

The Wingfield apartment faces an alley in a lower-middle-class St. Louis tenement. There is a fire escape with a landing and a screen on which words or images periodically appear. Tom Wingfield steps onstage dressed as a merchant sailor and speaks directly to the audience. According to the stage directions, Tom "takes whatever license with dramatic convention is convenient to his purposes." He explains the social and historical background of the play: the time is the late 1930s, when the American working classes are still reeling from the effects of the Great Depression. The civil war in Spain has just led to a massacre of civilians at Guernica. Tom also describes his role in the play and describes the other characters. One character, Tom's father, does not appear onstage: he abandoned the family years ago and, except for a terse postcard from Mexico, has not been heard from since. However, a picture of him hangs in the living room.

Tom enters the apartment's dining room, where Amanda, his mother, and Laura, his sister, are eating. Amanda calls Tom to the dinner table and, once he sits down, repeatedly tells him to chew his food. Laura rises to fetch something, but Amanda insists that she sit down and keep herself fresh for gentlemen callers. Amanda then launches into what is clearly an oft-recited account of the Sunday afternoon when she entertained seventeen gentlemen callers in her home in Blue Mountain, Mississippi. At Laura's urging, Tom listens attentively and asks his mother what appear to be habitual questions. Oblivious to his condescending tone, Amanda catalogues the men and their subsequent fates, how much money they left their widows, and how one suitor died carrying her picture.

Laura explains that no gentlemen callers come for her, since she is not as popular as her mother once was. Tom groans. Laura tells Tom that their mother is afraid that Laura will end up an old maid. The lights dim as what the stage directions term "the 'Glass Menagerie' music" plays.

SUMMARY: SCENE TWO

An image of blue roses appears on the screen as the scene begins. Laura is polishing her collection of glass figurines as Amanda, with a stricken face, walks up the steps outside. When Laura hears Amanda, she hides her ornaments and pretends to be studying a diagram of a keyboard. Amanda tears up the keyboard diagram and explains that she stopped by Rubicam's Business College, where Laura is supposedly enrolled. A teacher there informed her that Laura has not come to class since the first few days, when she suffered from terrible nervousness and became physically ill. Laura admits that she has been skipping class and explains that she has spent her days walking along the streets of winter, going to the zoo, and occasionally watching movies.

Amanda wonders what will become of the family now that Laura's prospects of a business career are ruined. She tells Laura that the only alternative is for Laura to get married. Amanda asks her if she has ever liked a boy. Laura tells her that, in high school, she had a crush on a boy named Jim, the school hero, who sat near her in the chorus. Laura tells her mother that once she told Jim that she had been away from school due to an attack of pleurosis. Because he misheard the name of the disease, he began calling her "Blue Roses." Laura notes that at graduation time he was engaged, and she speculates that he must be married by now. Amanda declares that Laura will nonetheless end up married to someone nice. Laura reminds her mother, apologetically, that she is "crippled"—that one of her legs is shorter than the other. Amanda insists that her daughter never use that word and tells her that she must cultivate charm.

ANALYSIS: SCENES ONE & TWO

With Tom's direct address to the audience, describing the play and the other characters, the play acknowledges its status as a work of art and admits that it does not represent reality. Tom's address also identifies the bias inherent in the portrayal of events that have already occurred: everything the audience sees will be filtered through Tom's memory and be subject to all of its guesswork, colorings, and subconscious distortions. The idea of a play with an involved narrator is not a new one. For instance, the Chorus in classical tragedy frequently plays a role much like Tom's, commenting on the actions as they occur. But these Choruses are seldom composed of characters who also play a part in the action. The presence of a character who both narrates and participates in the play is quite unusual, and Tom's dual role creates certain conflicts in his characterization. As narrator, Tom recounts and comments on the action from an unspecified date in the future and, as such, has acquired a certain emotional distance from the action. As a character, however, Tom is emotionally and physically involved in the action. Thus, Tom first appears as a cool, objective narrator who earns the audience's trust, but within minutes, he changes into an irritable young man embroiled in a petty argument with his mother over how he chews his food. As a consequence, the audience is never quite sure how to react to Tom—whether to take his opinions as the solid pronouncements of a narrator or the self-centered perspective of just another character.

Williams's production notes and stage directions emphasize his innovative theatrical vision. He felt that realism, which aimed to present life as it was without idealizing it, had outlived its usefulness. It offered, as Tom puts it, "illusion that has the appearance of truth." Williams sought the opposite in *The Glass Menagerie*: truth disguised as illusion. To accomplish this reversal of realism, the play employs elaborate visual and audio effects and expressionistic sets that emphasize symbolic meaning at the expense of realism. To underscore the illusions of the play, Tom makes a point of acknowledging these devices during his monologues as narrator.

Among the most striking effects in the play is the screen on which words or images that relate to the onstage action appear. The impression that this device creates on paper is sometimes confusing. In fact, the director of the original Broadway production of *The Glass Menagerie* chose to eliminate the screen from the performance. Sometimes the screen is used to emphasize the importance of something referred to by the characters, as when an image of blue roses appears in Scene Two as Laura recounts Jim's nickname for her. Sometimes it refers to something from a character's past or fantasy, as when Jim appears as a high school hero in the same scene, and sometimes it provides what seems like commentary from a witty outsider, as with "Ou sont les neiges d'antan?" in Scene One ("Ou sont les neiges . . ." is the title of a poem in praise of beautiful women by the fifteenth-century French poet François Villon). At times, the very obviousness of the symbols or themes that the screen emphasizes gives an ironic tone to the device. Like Tom's speeches, it reminds the audience of the importance of literary gimmicks and tricks in the creation of what the audience is seeing.

SCENE THREE

SUMMARY

The words "After the fiasco—" appear on the screen as the scene opens. Tom stands on the fire escape landing and addresses the audience. He explains that in the wake of what Tom refers to as the "fiasco" with Laura's college attendance, Amanda has become obsessed with procuring a gentleman caller for Laura. The image of a young man at the house with flowers appears on the screen. Tom says that in order to make a little extra money and thereby increase the family's ability to entertain suitors, Amanda runs a telephone subscription campaign for a magazine called *The Homemaker's Companion.*

The cover of a glamour magazine appears on the screen, and Amanda enters with a telephone. She makes a cheerful, elaborate, unsuccessful sales pitch to an acquaintance on the telephone, and then the lights dim. When they come up again, Tom and Amanda are engaged in a loud argument while Laura looks on desperately. Tom is enraged because his mother affords him no privacy and, furthermore, has returned the D. H. Lawrence novel he was reading to the library. She states that she will not permit that kind of "filth" in her house. Tom points out that he pays the rent and attempts to end the conversation by leaving the apartment. Amanda insists that Tom hear her out. She attributes his surly attitude to the fact that he spends every night out—doing something shameful, in her opinion—though he insists that he spends his nights at the movies. Amanda asserts that, by coming home late and depriving himself of sleep, he is endangering his job and, therefore, the family's security. Tom responds with a fierce outburst. He expresses his hatred for the factory, and he claims to envy the dead whenever he hears Amanda's daily call of "Rise and Shine!" He points out how he goes to work each day nonetheless and brings home the pay, how he has put aside all his dreams, and, if he truly were as selfish as Amanda claims, how he would have left long ago, just like his father.

Tom makes a move toward the door. Amanda demands to know where he is going. When she does not accept his response that he is going to the movies, he declares sarcastically that she is right and that he spends his nights at the lairs of criminals, opium houses, and casinos. He concludes his speech by calling Amanda an "ugly—babbling old—*witch*" and then grabs his coat. The coat resists his clumsy attempts to put it on, so he throws it to the other side of the room, where it hits Laura's glass menagerie, her collection of glass animal figurines. Glass breaks, and Laura utters a cry and turns away. The words "The Glass Menagerie" appear on the screen. Barely noticing the broken menagerie, Amanda declares she will not speak to Tom until she receives an apology. Tom bends down to pick up the glass and glances at Laura as if he would like to say something but says nothing. The "Glass Menagerie" music plays as the scene ends.

ANALYSIS

By the end of Scene Three, Williams has established the personalities of each of the three Wingfields and the conflicts that engage them. Tom's frustration with his job and home life, Amanda's nostalgia for her past and demands for the family's future, and Laura's social and physical handicaps all emerge quickly through the dialogue. There is almost no down time in the play because every scene is dominated by heightened emotions like anger and disillusionment or by major issues in the characters' lives, such as Laura's marriage prospects. The play always presents characters with measured ambiguity: each of them is deeply flawed, yet none is completely unsympathetic.

Amanda comes the closest to being a genuine antagonist. Her constant nagging suffocates and wounds her children, and her pettiness decreases her credibility in the eyes of her children and the audience. For example, her complaints about Tom's nighttime excursions may be legitimate, but they get lost in the reproaches she heaps upon him for his eating habits. Yet the hardship of her life as a single mother inspires sympathy. Her magazine subscription campaign is humiliating work, but it is a sacrifice and indignity that she is willing to undergo out of concern for her daughter's eventual happiness.

Mr. Wingfield's photograph hangs over everything that occurs onstage, indicating that, though the family has not seen him for years, he still plays a crucial role in their lives. Tom has been forced to adopt his absent father's role of breadwinner, and he is both tantalized and haunted by the idea that he might eventually adopt his father's role as deserter. Tom voices this possibility explicitly at the end of Scene Three, and we suspect that this occasion is not the first time he has done so. In fact, Amanda's apparently intrusive and unjustified concern with what her son reads and where he goes at night may stem from her awareness of this possibility. Her husband left her, we learn, because he "fell in love with long distances." With that in mind, it seems perfectly reasonable that she should be suspicious whenever Tom strays, mentally or physically, into any world outside their cramped apartment. The landing on the fire escape, where Tom is seen standing in Scene Three, ominously represents just what its name suggests: a route of escape from the "slow and implacable fires of human desperation" that burn steadily in the Wingfield household.

Close-knit, dysfunctional families are among Williams's favorite subjects, and the subject matter of *The Glass Menagerie* is closely connected to Williams's own life. Williams (whose real name was Thomas) spent a number of difficult years in St. Louis with his family, and for some of that time, he worked in a shoe factory. As a child, he was very close to his older sister, Rose, who, like Laura, was delicate and absorbed in fantasy. Rose even kept a collection of glass animals. As an adult, Rose was diagnosed with schizophrenia and eventually underwent a lobotomy in 1937. Williams never forgave his mother, a domineering former Southern belle like Amanda, for ordering the procedure. The use of "Blue Roses" as a nickname and symbol for Laura in her happiest moments (which quickly turn painful) is an explicit tribute to Rose Williams.

SCENE FOUR

You know it don't take much intelligence to get yourself into a nailed-up coffin, Laura. But who in hell ever got himself out of one without removing one nail?
(See QUOTATIONS, p. 43)

SUMMARY

A bell tolls five times as Tom returns home. He has been drinking. After painstakingly extracting his key from a jumble of cast-off items in his pockets, he drops it into a crack on the fire-escape landing. Laura hears him fumbling about and opens the door. He tells her that he has been at the movies for most of the night and also to a magic show, in which the magician changed water to wine to beer to whiskey. Tom then gives Laura a rainbow-colored scarf, which he says the magician gave to him. He describes how the magician allowed himself to be nailed into a coffin and escaped without removing a nail. Tom remarks wryly that the same trick could come in handy for him but wonders how one could possibly get out of a coffin without removing a single nail. Mr. Wingfield's photograph lights up, presenting an example of someone who has apparently performed such a feat. The lights dim.

At six in the morning, Amanda calls out her habitual "Rise and Shine!" This time, though, she tells Laura to pass the message on to Tom because Amanda refuses to talk to Tom until he apologizes. Laura gets Tom out of bed and implores him to apologize to their mother. He remains reluctant. Amanda then sends Laura out to buy groceries on credit. On the way down the fire escape, Laura slips and falls but is not hurt. Several moments of silence pass in the dining room before Tom rises from the table and apologizes. Amanda nearly breaks into tears, and Tom speaks gently to her. She speaks of her pride in her children and begs Tom to promise her that he will never be a drunkard. She then turns the discussion to Laura as the "Glass Menagerie" music begins to play. Amanda has caught Laura crying because Laura thinks that Tom is not happy living with them and that he goes out every night to escape the apartment. Amanda claims to understand that Tom has greater ambitions than the warehouse, but she also expresses her worry at seeing him stay out late, just as his father, a heavy drinker, used to do. She questions Tom again about where he goes at night, and Tom says that he goes to the movies for adventure, which, he laments, is so absent from his career and life in general. At the mention of the word "adventure," a sailing vessel appears on the screen. "Man is by instinct a lover, a hunter, a fighter," Tom says, and he points out that the warehouse does not offer him the chance to be any of those things. Amanda does not want to hear about instinct. She considers it the function of animals and not a concern of "Christian adults."

Tom is impatient to get to work, but Amanda holds him back to talk about her worry over Laura's future. Amanda has tried to integrate Laura into the rest of the world by enrolling her in business college and taking her to Young People's League meetings at church, but nothing has worked. Laura is unable to speak to people outside her family and spends all her time with old records and her glass menagerie. Amanda tells Tom that she knows that he has gotten a letter from the merchant marine and is itching to leave, but she asks him to wait until Laura has someone to take care of her. She then asks him to find some decent man at the warehouse and bring him home to meet Laura. Heading down the fire escape, Tom reluctantly agrees. Amanda makes another call for the magazine subscription drive, and then the lights fade.

ANALYSIS

For the first production of *The Glass Menagerie,* the composer Paul Bowles wrote a musical theme entitled "The Glass Menagerie." This music plays when Amanda discusses Laura at the breakfast table with Tom and at other crucial moments involving Laura. The title and timing of the music equate Laura with her glass animals. Like the objects that she loves so well, Laura is incredibly delicate (a typing drill is enough to make her physically ill) and oddly fanciful. Somehow, the fights and struggles that shape Amanda's and Tom's lives have not hardened Laura. Amanda and Tom argue constantly about their respective responsibilities to the family, but Laura never joins in. Interestingly, Laura does not participate in supporting the family and, though Amanda is upset when Laura deceives her about the business college, neither Tom nor Amanda resents Laura's dependence in any way. Her physical and resultant emotional disabilities seem to excuse her from any practical obligation to the household.

Though she does nothing to hold the family together financially, Laura holds it together emotionally. Amanda hits on this truth when she reminds Tom that he cannot leave as long as Laura depends on him. Both Tom and Amanda are capable of working to support themselves, and, without the childlike Laura, this family of three adults would almost certainly dissolve. In addition, Laura's role as peacemaker proves crucial to ending the standoff between Tom and Amanda. Laura valiantly tries to douse the "slow and implacable fires" of her family's unhappiness—to play firefighter, in a sense. Interestingly, she trips on the fire escape when she leaves the apartment. This event contributes to the reconciliation between Tom and Amanda, who are united in their concern for Laura, and it also draws attention to the fact that, for Laura, escape from the emotional fires of her family is impossible. Thus, she has no choice but to do everything she can to extinguish them.

The closeness and warmth of Tom's relationship with Laura becomes evident when Tom comes home drunk at the beginning of Scene Four. In general, when Amanda is around, she tends to dominate the conversation, and the siblings can exchange very few words exclusive to the two of them. Here, though, they are alone. Laura's love and concern for Tom are great enough to prompt her to wake up at five in the morning to see if he has come home. Tom uses his account of the magic show to share his most intimate experiences and thoughts with Laura. He subtly confesses to her about his drinking when he talks about the magician turning water to whiskey. Then, the coffin anecdote reveals both Tom's sense of morbid confinement in his job and family life and his impossible dreams of escaping the family "without removing one nail"—that is, without destroying it. A number of critics have suggested that Tom feels an incestuous romantic attachment to Laura. This theory is supported by the subtly presented intensity of the relationship between these two young adults, both of whom are, in their different ways, incapable of establishing complete lives outside their family.

The imagery in Tom's speech about the magic show contains several layers of symbolic meaning. The coffin trick, with its suggestions of rising from the dead, is a reference to Christian resurrection. Christian themes are also suggested by Tom's tendency, when he reaches the limits of his patience with Amanda's reproaches, to see himself as a martyr committing a supreme sacrifice for the family's good. In addition, the rainbow-colored scarf that Tom brings home and gives to Laura reminds the audience of the rainbow of colors refracted by her glass animals. On a social and historical front, the coffin is representative of the condition of the American lower middle classes, whom Williams describes, in the stage directions, as a "fundamentally enslaved" sector of America.

SCENE FIVE

SUMMARY

The screen reads "Annunciation." Some time has passed since the last scene, and it is now the spring of 1937. Amanda and Laura clear the table after dinner. Amanda nags Tom about his disheveled appearance and his smoking habits. Tom steps onto the fire-escape landing and addresses the audience, describing what he remembers about the area where he grew up. There was a dance hall across the alley, he tells us, from which music emanated on spring evenings. Rainbow refractions from the hall's glass ball were visible through the Wingfields' windows, and young couples kissed in the alley. Tom says that the way youth entertained themselves at the dance hall was a natural reaction to lives that, like his own, lacked "any change or adventure." He notes, however, that his peers would soon be offered all the adventure they wanted as America prepared to enter World War II.

Amanda joins Tom on the landing. They speak more gently than before, and each makes a wish on the moon. Tom refuses to tell what his wish is, and Amanda says that she wishes for the success and happiness of her children. Tom announces that there will be a gentleman caller: he has asked a nice young man from the warehouse to dinner. Amanda is thrilled, and Tom reveals that the caller will be coming the next day. This information agitates Amanda, who is overwhelmed by all the preparations that will need to be made before then. Tom tells her not to make a fuss, but he cannot stem the tide of her excitement. As she leads Tom back inside, Amanda frets about the linen, the silver, new curtains, chintz covers, and a new floor lamp, all the while despairing the lack of time to repaper the walls.

Amanda proceeds to brush Tom's hair while interrogating him about the young gentleman caller. Her first concern is that he not be a drunkard. Tom thinks she is being a bit hasty in assuming that Laura will marry the visitor. Amanda continues to press him for information and learns that the caller, who is named Jim O'Connor, is a shipping clerk at the warehouse. Tom reveals that both sides of Jim's family are Irish and that Jim makes eighty-five dollars a month. Jim is neither ugly nor too good-looking, and he goes to night school to study radio engineering and public speaking and is a proponent of self-improvement. Amanda is pleased by what she hears, particularly about his ambition. Tom warns her that Jim does not know that he has been invited specifically to meet Laura, stating that he offered Jim only a simple, unqualified invitation to dinner. This news does not matter to Amanda, who is sure that Laura will dazzle Jim. Tom asks her not to expect too much of Laura. He reminds Amanda that Laura is crippled, socially odd, and lives in a fantasy world. To outsiders who do not love her as family, Tom insists, Laura must seem peculiar. Amanda begs him not to use words like "crippled" and "peculiar" and asserts that Laura is strange in a good way.

Tom gets up to leave. Amanda demands to know where he is going. He replies that he is going to the movies and leaves despite his mother's objections. Amanda is troubled, but her excitement quickly returns. She calls Laura out onto the landing and tells her to make a wish on the moon. Laura does not know what she should wish for. Amanda, overcome with emotion, tells her to wish for happiness and good fortune.

ANALYSIS

Although Amanda seems to do everything she can to make her children happy, many of her expectations of what will make them happy are actually egocentric—that is, they are based on Amanda's own definition of happiness. Amanda claims to value her children's well-being above her own, and in some ways her behavior supports that claim. She does, for example, subject herself to the pedestrian work of subscription-selling in order to help Laura find a husband. Yet Amanda's nagging of Tom and her refusal to recognize Laura's flaws indicate her deep-rooted selfishness. She wants the best for Tom and Laura, but her concept of the best has far more to do with her own values than with her children's interests and dreams. Tom wants intellectual stimulation and a literary life, and Amanda refuses to admit that these may provide as valid a vision of happiness as financial stability. Gentleman callers hold no interest for Laura, but they hold great interest for Amanda, who refuses to accept that her daughter is not identical to her in this regard.

There is much to condemn in Amanda's selfishness. However, the trajectory of her life also offers much to pity. Amanda simply cannot accept her transition from pampered Southern belle to struggling single mother. Some of her richest dialogue occurs when the genteel manners of her past come to the surface—when she calls the moon a "little silver slipper" or bursts out with a string of Southern endearments in her subscription-drive phone calls. Such elegant turns of phrase seem tragically out of place in a St. Louis tenement.

The figure of the fallen Southern belle is based loosely on Williams's own mother, who grew up in a prominent Mississippi family and suffered reversals of fortune in her adulthood. This figuration remains one of the best-known trademarks of Williams's plays—Blanche DuBois in *A Streetcar Named Desire* is perhaps the most famous representative of this type. The social and historical circumstances surrounding characters like Amanda point to some of the broader concerns of *The Glass Menagerie*. In the decades after the Civil War, many once-distinguished Southern families saw their economic fortunes decline. Daughters of these families, like Amanda, traditionally were raised to take pride in their social status. In a rapidly industrializing and modernizing America, however, that status was worth less and less. New money was seen as far more desirable than old but penniless family grandeur. The promise of Amanda's past remains unfulfilled and always will remain so, but she refuses to accept this fact and convinces herself, wrongly, that Laura can still live the life that she expected for herself. At the end of the play, Amanda chides Tom for being a "dreamer." It is clear, however, that the Wingfield children's inability to deal with reality is inherited directly from their mother.

In Scene Five, Amanda's far-fetched dreams for Laura appear to be within reach. The screen legend at the beginning of the scene is "Annunciation"—a word that, besides simply meaning "announcement," also refers to the Catholic celebration of God's announcement to the Virgin Mary that she is pregnant with Jesus Christ. Jim, then, may be seen as a savior—for Laura and for the entire family. Furthermore, Amanda's description of the moon as a "little silver slipper" also calls to mind the Cinderella fairy tale, which Williams considered an important story. In one version of this tale, a handsome young prince rescues a maiden from a lifetime of domestic drudgery, and a glass slipper is crucial to cementing the match. Amanda's hopes for Jim's visit are high, and clues such as the slipper suggest that they may be correctly so. Soon, though, Williams's references to the birth of a savior and of fairy-tale romance are revealed as ironic omens of tragedy.

Scene Six

I married no planter! I married a man who worked for the telephone company! . . . A telephone man who— fell in love with long-distance!

(See QUOTATIONS, *p. 40*)

Summary
Tom leans against the rail of the fire-escape landing, smoking, as the lights come up. He addresses the audience, recollecting the background of the gentleman caller. In high school, Jim O'Connor was a star in everything he did—an athlete, a singer, a debater, the leader of his class—and everyone was certain that he would go far. Yet things did not turn out according to expectations. Six years out of high school, Jim was working a job that was hardly better than Tom's. Tom remembers that he and Jim were on friendly terms. As the only one at the warehouse who knew about Jim's past glories, Tom was useful to Jim. Jim called Tom "Shakespeare" because of his habit of writing poems in the warehouse bathroom when work was slow.

Tom's soliloquy ends, and the lights come up on a living room transformed by Amanda's efforts over the past twenty-four hours. Amanda adjusts Laura's new dress. Laura is nervous and uncomfortable with all the fuss that is being made, but Amanda assures her that it is only right for a girl to aim to trap a man with her beauty. When Laura is ready, Amanda goes to dress herself and then makes a grand entrance wearing a dress from her youth. She recalls wearing that same dress to a cotillion (a formal ball, often for debutantes) in Mississippi, to the Governor's Ball, and to receive her gentlemen callers. Finally, her train of memories leads her to recollections of Mr. Wingfield.

Amanda mentions Jim's name, and Laura realizes that the visitor is the same young man on whom she had a crush in high school. She panics, claiming that she will not be able to eat at the same table with him. Amanda dismisses Laura's terror and busies herself in the kitchen making salmon for dinner. When the doorbell rings, Amanda calls for Laura to get it, but Laura desperately begs her mother to open it instead. When Amanda refuses, Laura at last opens the door, awkwardly greets Jim, and then retreats to the record player. Tom explains to Jim that she is extremely shy, and Jim remarks, "It's unusual to meet a shy girls nowadays."

Jim and Tom talk while the women are elsewhere. Jim encourages Tom to join him in the public speaking course he is taking. Jim is sure that he and Tom were both meant for executive jobs and that "social poise" is the only determinant of success. However, Jim also warns Tom that, if Tom does not wake up, the boss will soon fire Tom at the warehouse. Tom says that his own plans have nothing to do with public speaking or executive positions and that he is planning a big change in his life. Jim, bewildered, asks what he means, and Tom explains vaguely that he is sick of living vicariously through the cinema. He is bored with "the *movies*" and wants "to *move*," he says. Unbeknownst to Amanda, he has taken the money intended to pay for that month's electric bill and used it to join the Union of Merchant Seamen. Tom announces rather proudly that he is taking after his father.

Amanda enters, talking gaily and laying on the Southern charm as she introduces herself to Jim. She praises Laura to him and, within minutes, gives him a general account of her numerous girlhood suitors and her failed marriage. Amanda sends Tom to fetch Laura for dinner, but Tom returns to say that Laura is feeling ill and does not want to eat. A storm begins outside. Amanda calls Laura herself, and Laura enters, stumbling and letting out a moan just as a clap of thunder explodes. Seeing that Laura is truly ill, Amanda tells her to rest on the sofa in the living room. Amanda, Jim, and Tom sit down at the table, where Amanda glances anxiously at Jim while Tom says grace. Laura, in the living room alone, struggles to contain a sob.

ANALYSIS

Laura's glasslike qualities become more explicit in Scene Six, where, according to the stage directions, she resembles "glass touched by light, given a momentary radiance." She embodies the "momentary radiance" of glass more completely in Scene Seven. Here, however, it is the fragility of glass that is most evident in her character. Before now, we have merely heard about the panic that results from her shyness. In this scene, we witness it directly, as her reason breaks down in the face of the terror that Jim's presence instills in her.

The straightforward, iron-willed Jim contrasts sharply with the elusive, delicate Laura. Jim is, as Tom says in Scene One, a representative from the "world of reality." His entrance marks the first time in the play that the audience comes into contact with the outside world from which the Wingfields, in their various ways, are all hiding. As embodied by Jim, that world seems brash, bland, and almost vulgar. His confidence and good cheer never waver. He offers Tom, and later Laura, a steady stream of clichés about success, self-confidence, and progress. Whereas Laura's life is built around glass, Jim plans to build his around the "social poise" that consists of knowing how to use words to influence people.

Jim is as different from the rest of the Wingfields as he is from Laura. Whereas Tom sees the warehouse as a coffin, Jim sees it as the starting point of his career. For Jim, it is the entrance to a field in which he will attain commercial success, the only kind of success that he can perceive. Amanda lives in a past riddled with traditions and gentility, while Jim looks only toward the future of science, technology, and business. Given these contrasts, one might expect Jim to be bewildered and disgusted by the Wingfields and to be repulsed by the claustrophobia and dysfunction of their household. Instead, he is generous with them. He is good-natured about Tom's ambivalent performance at his job, and most important, he is charmed by Laura's imagination and vulnerability. Given Jim's philosophy of life and belief in the value of social grace, it is possible that his remarkable tolerance and understanding is not a result of genuine compassion but, rather, an expression of the belief that it is always in one's best interest to try to get along with everyone.

While Jim's presence emphasizes the alienation of the Wingfields from the rest of the world, it simultaneously lends a new dignity and comprehensibility to that alienation. Jim's professed dreams present a nightmare vision of the impersonality of humanity—shallow, materialistic, and blindly, relentlessly upbeat. We are forced to consider the question of whether it is preferable to live in a world of Wingfields or a world of Jims. There is no easy answer to this question, but it seems possible that, for all their unhappiness, Amanda and Tom would choose the former because the Wingfields' world is emotionally richer than Jim's. Along these lines, it seems possible that the outside world has not so much rejected the Wingfields as they have rejected the outside world.

Scene Seven

Oh, be careful—if you breathe, it breaks!
(See QUOTATIONS, p. 41)

Summary

A half hour later, dinner is winding down. Laura is still by herself on the living-room couch. The floor lamp gives her face an ethereal beauty. As the rain stops, the lights flicker and go out. Amanda lights candles and asks Jim to check the fuses, but of course, he finds nothing wrong with them. Amanda then asks Tom if he paid the electric bill. He admits that he did not, and she assumes that he simply forgot, as Jim's good humor helps smooth over the potentially tense moment. Amanda sends Jim to the parlor with a candelabra and a little wine to keep Laura company while Amanda and Tom clean up.

In the living room, Jim takes a seat on the floor and persuades Laura to join him. He gives her a glass of wine. Tongue-tied at first, Laura soon relaxes in Jim's engaging presence. He talks to her about the Century of Progress exhibition in Chicago and calls her an "old-fashioned" girl. She reminds him that they knew each other in high school. He has forgotten, but when she mentions the nickname he gave her, Blue Roses, he remembers. They reminisce about high school and Jim's glories. Laura also remembers the discomfort and embarrassment she felt over the brace on her leg. Jim tells her that she was far too self-conscious and that everybody has problems.

Laura persuades him to sign a program from a play he performed in during high school, which she has kept, and works up the nerve to ask him about the girl to whom he was supposedly engaged. He explains that he was never actually engaged and that the girl had announced the engagement out of wishful thinking.

In response to his question about what she has done since high school, Laura starts to tell Jim about her glass collection. He abruptly declares that she has an inferiority complex and that she "low-rates" herself. He says that he also suffered from this condition after his post–high school disappointment. He launches into his vision of his own future in television production. Laura listens attentively. He asks her about herself again, and she describes her collection of glass animals. She shows him her favorite: a unicorn. He points out lightly that unicorns are "extinct" in modern times.

Jim notices the music coming from the dance hall across the alley. Despite Laura's initial protests, he leads her in a clumsy waltz around the room. Jim bumps into the table where the unicorn is resting, the unicorn falls, and its horn breaks off. Laura is unfazed, though, and she says that now the unicorn can just be a regular horse. Extremely apologetic, Jim tells her that she is different from anyone else he knows, that she is pretty, and that if she were his sister he would teach her to have some self-confidence and value her own uniqueness. He then says that someone ought to kiss her.

Jim kisses Laura on the lips. Dazed, Laura sinks down onto the sofa. He immediately begins chiding himself out loud for what he has done. As he sits next to her on the sofa, Jim confesses that he is involved with an Irish girl named Betty, and he tells her that his love for Betty has made a new man of him. Laura places the de-horned unicorn in his hand, telling him to think of it as a souvenir.

Amanda enters in high spirits, carrying refreshments. Jim quickly becomes awkward in her presence. She insists that he become a frequent caller from now on. He says he must leave now and explains that he has to pick up Betty at the train station—the two of them are to be married in June. Despite her disappointment, Amanda bids him farewell graciously. Jim cheerily takes his leave.

Amanda calls Tom in from the kitchen and accuses him of playing a joke on them. Tom insists that he had no idea that Jim was engaged and that he does not know much about anyone at the warehouse. He heads to the door, intending to spend another night at the movies. Amanda accuses him of being a "dreamer" and rails against his selfishness as he leaves. Tom returns her scolding. Amanda tells him that he might as well go not just to the movies but to the moon, for all that he cares about her and Laura. Tom leaves, slamming the door.

Tom delivers his passionate closing monologue from the fire-escape landing as Amanda inaudibly comforts Laura inside the apartment and then withdraws to her room. Tom explains that he was fired soon after from the warehouse for writing a poem on a shoebox lid and that he then left the family. He says that he has traveled for a long time, pursuing something he cannot identify. But he has found that he cannot leave Laura behind. No matter where he goes, some piece of glass or quality of light makes it seem as if his sister is at his side. In the living room, Laura blows the candles out as Tom bids her goodbye.

> Oh, Laura, Laura, I tried to leave you behind me, but I am more faithful than I intended to be!
> (See QUOTATIONS, p. 43)

ANALYSIS

As Scene Seven begins, Laura's face is made beautiful by the new floor lamp and its lampshade of "rose-colored silk." Williams marshals the force of metaphor through the accrued weight of symbols. The delicate light represents Laura, and the rose represents Laura, whom Jim used to call "Blue Roses." The glass unicorn that Jim breaks accidentally is yet another symbol that points to Laura. Like the unicorn, Laura is an impossible oddity. Jim's kindness and kiss bring her abruptly into the normal world by shattering the protective layer of glass that she has set up around herself, but this real world also involves heartbreak, which she suffers at Jim's hands.

Though Jim is an emissary from a very different world, he also shares some fundamental qualities with the Wingfields, each of whom is somehow unable to connect to the world around him or her. Jim seems to be well integrated into the outside world, to accept its philosophy of life, and to have latched onto a number of things that keep him afloat: public speaking, radio engineering, and Betty. But his long-winded speeches to Laura reveal an insecurity that he is fighting with all his might. He has somehow strayed off the glorious path on which he seemed destined to travel in high school. Lacking an inherent sense of self-worth, he is scrambling to find something that will give him such a sense. Jim talks as if he is trying to convince himself as much as all the others that he has the self-confidence he needs to succeed.

Each character in *The Glass Menagerie* is trying to escape from reality in his or her own way: Laura retreats into her imagination and the static world of glass animals and old records, Amanda has the glorious days of her youth, and Jim has his dreams of an executive position. Only Tom has trouble finding a satisfactory route of escape. Movies are not a real way out, as he comes to realize. Even descending the steps of the fire escape and wandering like his rootless father does not provide him with any respite from his memories of Laura's stunted life and crushed hopes. Yet, in one way, he *has* escaped. A frustrated poet no longer, he has created this play. Laura's act of blowing out the candles at the play's end signifies the snuffing of her hopes, but it may also mark Tom's long-awaited release from her grip. He exhorts Laura to blow out her candles and then bids her what sounds like a final goodbye. The play itself is Tom's way out, a cathartic attempt to purge his memory and free himself through the act of creation.

Even so, when one considers the trajectory of Tennessee Williams's life and writings, one senses a deep ambivalence in the play's conclusion. The rose image continued to show up in Williams's writings long after *The Glass Menagerie,* and the ghosts haunting Williams would eventually lead him to drug addiction and a mental hospital. For Williams and his character Tom, art may be an attempt to erase all pain. But although Williams's world includes some survivors of deep pain and torment, they invariably bear ugly scars.

IMPORTANT QUOTATIONS EXPLAINED

1. But the wonderfullest trick of all was the coffin trick.
    We nailed him into a coffin and he got out of the coffin
    without removing one nail. . . . There is a trick that would
    come in handy for me—get me out of this two-by-four
    situation! . . . You know it don't take much intelligence to
    get yourself into a nailed-up coffin, Laura. But who in hell
    ever got himself out of one without removing one nail?

At the beginning of Scene Four, Tom, returning home from the movies, tells Laura about a magic show in which the magician performs the coffin trick. Tom, who dreams of adventure and literary greatness but is tied down to a mindless job and a demanding family, sees the coffin as a symbol of his own life situation. He has been contemplating an escape from his private coffin since the beginning of the play, and at the end, he finally goes through with it, walking out on his family after he is fired from his job. But Tom's escape is not nearly as impressive as the magician's. Indeed, it consists of no fancier a trick than walking down the stairs of the fire escape. Nor is Tom's escape as seamless as the magician's. The magician gets out of the coffin without disturbing one nail, but Tom's departure is certain to have a major impact on the lives of Amanda and Laura. At the beginning of Scene One, Tom admits that he is "the opposite of a stage magician." The illusion of escape that the magician promotes is, in the end, out of Tom's reach.

2.   Well, in the South we had so many servants. Gone, gone,
      gone. All vestige of gracious living! Gone completely! I
      wasn't prepared for what the future brought me. All of my
      gentlemen callers were sons of planters and so of course
      I assumed that I would be married to one and raise my
      family on a large piece of land with plenty of servants. But
      man proposes—and woman accepts the proposal! To vary
      that old, old saying a bit—I married no planter! I married
      a man who worked for the telephone company! . . . A
      telephone man who—fell in love with long-distance!

This quote is drawn from Scene Six, as Amanda subjects Jim, who
has just arrived at the Wingfield apartment for dinner, to the full
force of her high-volume, girlish Southern charm. Within minutes
of meeting him, Amanda introduces Jim to the broad arc of her life
history: her much-lamented transition from pampered belle to deserted wife. As she does throughout the play, Amanda here equates
her own downfall with that of a system of "gracious living" associated with the Old South, which contrasts starkly with the vulgarity
and squalor of 1930s St. Louis. Naturally, Amanda's intense nostalgia for a bygone world may have something to do with the fact that
neither she nor her children have managed to succeed in the more
modern world in which they now live.

Amanda's memories of her multitudinous "gentlemen callers"
are responsible for the visit of Jim, whom Amanda sees as a com-
parable gentleman caller for Laura. Amanda's decision to tell Jim
immediately about her gentlemen callers demonstrates the high
hopes she has for his visit. Indeed, the speech quoted might be taken
as rather tactless move—a sign that Amanda's social graces have a
touch of hysterical thoughtlessness to them and that putting herself
and her story at the center of attention is more important to her than
creating a favorable atmosphere for Laura and Jim's meeting.

3. LAURA: Little articles of [glass], they're ornaments mostly!
Most of them are little animals made out of glass,
the tiniest little animals in the world. Mother calls
them a glass menagerie! Here's an example of one,
if you'd like to see it! . . . Oh, be careful—if you
breathe, it breaks! . . . You see how the light shines
through him?

JIM: It sure does shine!

LAURA: I shouldn't be partial, but he is my favorite one.

JIM: What kind of a thing is this one supposed to be?

LAURA: Haven't you noticed the single horn on his
forehead?

JIM: A unicorn, huh? —aren't they extinct in the modern
world?

LAURA: I know!

JIM: Poor little fellow, he must feel sort of lonesome.

This exchange occurs in Scene Seven, after Jim's warmth has enabled
Laura to overcome her shyness in his presence and introduce him
to the collection of glass animals that is her most prized possession.
By this point in the play, we are well aware that the glass menagerie
is a symbol for Laura herself. Here, she warns him about the ease
with which the glass figurines might be broken and shows him the
wonderful visions produced when they are held up to the right sort
of light. In doing so, she is essentially describing herself: exquisitely
delicate but glowing under the right circumstances.

The glass unicorn, Laura's favorite figurine, symbolizes her even
more specifically. The unicorn is different from ordinary horses, just
as Laura is different from other people. In fact, the unicorn is so
unusual a creature that Jim at first has trouble recognizing it. Unicorns are "extinct in the modern world," and similarly, Laura is ill-
adapted for survival in the world in which she lives. The loneliness
that Jim identifies in the lone unicorn is the same loneliness to which
Laura has resigned herself and from which Jim has the potential to
save her.

4. JIM: Aw, aw, aw. Is it broken?
    LAURA: Now it is just like all the other horses.
    JIM: It's lost its—
    LAURA: Horn! It doesn't matter. . . . [*smiling*] I'll just imagine
            he had an operation. The horn was removed to make
            him feel less—freakish!

This exchange, also from Scene Seven, occurs not long after the previous one. After persuading Laura to dance with him, Jim accidentally bumps the table on which the glass unicorn rests, breaking the horn off of the figurine. Apparently, Laura's warning to him about the delicacy of the glass objects reflects a very reasonable caution, but Jim fails to take the warning seriously enough. The accident with the unicorn foreshadows his mishandling of Laura, as he soon breaks her heart by announcing that he is engaged.

Just as Jim's clumsy advances make Laura seem and feel like an ordinary girl, his clumsy dancing turns her beloved unicorn into an ordinary horse. For the time being, Laura is optimistic about the change, claiming that the unicorn should be happy to feel like less of a misfit, just as she herself is temporarily happy because Jim's interest in her makes her feel like less of an outcast. Laura and the glass unicorn have similar fragility, however, and Laura, perhaps knowingly, predicts her own fate when she implies that no matter how careful Jim might be, her hopes will end up shattered.

5.   I descended the steps of this fire escape for a last time
        and followed, from then on, in my father's footsteps,
        attempting to find in motion what was lost in space. . . . I
        would have stopped, but I was pursued by something. . . .
        I pass the lighted window of a shop where perfume is
        sold. The window is filled with pieces of colored glass,
        tiny transparent bottles in delicate colors, like bits of a
        shattered rainbow. Then all at once my sister touches my
        shoulder. I turn around and look into her eyes. Oh, Laura,
        Laura, I tried to leave you behind me, but I am more
        faithful than I intended to be!

The play closes with this speech by Tom, at the end of Scene Seven. Here, Tom speaks as the narrator, from some point in time years after the action of the play. He describes how he leaves Amanda and Laura after being fired from his job and embarks on the life of the wanderer, just as his father did years ago. This escape is what Tom dreams of aloud in Scene Four, and it is Tom's chosen means of pursuing the "adventure" that he discusses with Amanda in Scene Four and Jim in Scene Six. From Tom's vague description of his fate after leaving home, it is unclear whether he has found adventure or not. What is clear is that his escape is an imperfect, incomplete one. Memories of Laura chase him wherever he goes, and those memories prove as confining as the Wingfield apartment.

Tom's statement that "I am more faithful than I intended to be!" indicates that Tom is fully aware that deserting his family was a faithless and morally reprehensible act, and the guilt associated with it may have something to do with his inability to leave Laura fully behind. But the word "faithful" also has strong associations with the language of lovers. A number of critics have suggested that Tom's character is influenced by an incestuous desire for Laura. The language used in this sentence and the hold that Laura maintains over Tom's memory help to support this theory.

KEY FACTS

FULL TITLE
The Glass Menagerie

AUTHOR
Tennessee Williams (born Thomas Lanier Williams III)

TYPE OF WORK
Play

GENRE
Tragedy; family drama

LANGUAGE
English

TIME AND PLACE WRITTEN
1941–1943; a number of American cities, including New York, St. Louis, and Los Angeles

DATE OF FIRST PUBLICATION
1945

PUBLISHER
Random House

NARRATOR
Tom Wingfield

POINT OF VIEW
Tom both narrates and participates in the play. The older Tom remembers his youth and then becomes a younger Tom who participates in the action as scenes from his youth play out. The point of view of the older Tom is reflective, and he warns us that his memory distorts the past. The younger Tom is impulsive and angry. The action sometimes consists of events that Tom does not witness; at these points, the play goes beyond simply describing events from Tom's own memory.

TONE
Tragic; sarcastic; bleak

TENSE

The play uses both the present and past tenses. The older Tom speaks in the past tense about his recollections, and the younger Tom takes part in a play that occurs in the present tense.

SETTING (TIME)

Tom, from an indefinite point in the future, remembers the winter and spring of 1937.

SETTING (PLACE)

An apartment in St. Louis

PROTAGONIST

Tom Wingfield

MAJOR CONFLICT

In their own ways, each of the Wingfields struggles against the hopelessness that threatens their lives. Tom's fear of working in a dead-end job for decades drives him to work hard creating poetry, which he finds more fulfilling. Amanda's disappointment at the fading of her glory motivates her attempts to make her daughter, Laura, more popular and social. Laura's extreme fear of seeing Jim O'Connor reveals her underlying concern about her physical appearance and about her inability to integrate herself successfully into society.

RISING ACTION

After Laura admits to leaving a business course that would have allowed her to get a job, her mother, Amanda, decides that Laura must get married; Tom tells Amanda that he is going to bring Jim O'Connor to dinner; Amanda prepares extensively, hoping that Jim will become Laura's suitor.

CLIMAX

Each character's struggle comes to a climax at different points. Tom's decision not to pay the electric bill and to use the money instead to leave his family in search of adventure reveals his initial, decisive break from his family struggles. When Jim breaks the horn from Laura's glass unicorn and announces that he is engaged, the possibility that he will help her overcome her self-doubt and shyness is also destroyed. When Amanda discovers that Jim is engaged, she loses her hope that Laura will attain the popularity and social standing that Amanda herself has lost.

FALLING ACTION

Laura gives Jim the broken unicorn as a souvenir; Jim leaves the house to pick up his girlfriend; Amanda accuses Tom of not having revealed that Jim was engaged. Addressing the audience, Tom explains that not long after that incident he left his family but was never able to emotionally leave Laura behind—in his later travels, he frequently felt a connection to her.

THEMES

The difficulty of accepting reality; the impossibility of true escape; the unrelenting power of memory

MOTIFS

Abandonment; the words and images on the screen; music

SYMBOLS

Laura's glass menagerie; the glass unicorn; "Blue Roses"; the fire escape

FORESHADOWING

Tom's departure is foreshadowed by his frequent retreats to the fire escape and the image of a sailing vessel on the screen; the music from the Paradise Dance Hall across the street foreshadows Laura and Jim's dancing; Jim's breaking of the unicorn foreshadows his breaking of her heart.

STUDY QUESTIONS

1. *Tom calls Laura "peculiar," but Amanda bristles at this word. What is "peculiar" about Laura?*

When Amanda asks Tom to explain what he means when he calls Laura "peculiar," he refers to the fact that she never goes out and says that "[s]he lives in a world of her own—a world of little glass ornaments." Her inability to talk to strangers is also unusual, as is the violent illness that overtakes her when she is faced with the most minimal of social pressures. One of her legs is shorter than the other, and it is quite possible that this physical deformity contributes to her pathological shyness. Jim suggests another possible explanation for her oddity: he believes that all of her peculiarities stem from an inferiority complex and that they would disappear if she could only learn to think more highly of herself. Another more complex explanation for Laura's odd behavior is that she lives in a fantasy world of her own creation. Like the glass menagerie, this fantasy world is dangerously delicate. Because direct contact with the real world threatens to shatter Laura's fantasies, much as the touch of any solid object will pop a soap bubble, she is terrified of any interaction with reality. If such is the case, then Laura begins to look a little less *peculiar*. After all, Amanda and Tom also live to some extent in fantasy worlds—Amanda in the past and Tom in movies and literature. The only difference between Laura and them, perhaps, is that she inhabits her fantasy world much more completely than they inhabit theirs.

A single line from Laura reveals the complexity of the question of exactly how peculiar she is. In Scene Seven, she says to Jim that she has never heard her glass horses argue among themselves. If we are meant to believe that she actually expects the glass figures to talk, then this quote demonstrates that she is deeply and unhealthily engrossed in her fantasies. Yet the stage directions indicate that she should say this line "lightly." It seems that she is just making a joke, which would indicate that she can, on the right occasion, distance herself enough from her fantasy world to find humor and absurdity in it.

49

2.   *Why is the fire escape important in the play?*

On the most concrete level, the fire escape is an emblem of the Wing-fields' poverty. In Amanda's youth, she would have stepped onto a veranda or a porch for fresh air. But she and her children now live in a tenement in an urban center, and outdoor space is hard to come by. Yet in Scene Five, in one of the play's few cautiously optimistic moments, the Wingfields still manage to find romance and hope on the fire escape, when Tom and Amanda wish on the moon. The fire escape also represents exactly what the name implies: the promise of escape from the overheated atmosphere of the apartment. Williams describes life in these tenements as the constant burning of the "slow and implacable fires of human desperation." Tom, for one, is suffocated by the heat of these fires and occasionally steps onto the fire-escape landing to have a smoke. "I'm starting to boil inside," he tells Jim in Scene Six. The photo of Mr. Wingfield operates with the fire escape to remind Tom and the audience that leaving is possible, and at the end of the play, Tom does indeed walk down the fire escape steps, never to return. Yet this possibility does not exist for everyone. In Scene Five, Laura slips and falls on the fire escape while on her way to a nearby store. For her, escape is impossible, and the fire escape, which takes the people she loves away from her, represents only the possibility of injury and destruction.

3.   *Which aspects of* THE GLASS MENAGERIE *are realistic? Which aspects are the most nonrealistic? What function do the nonrealistic elements serve?*

In the Production Notes to *The Glass Menagerie,* Williams writes disparagingly of the "straight realistic play with its genuine Frigidaire and authentic ice cubes." Generally, Williams found realism to be a flat, outdated, and insufficient way of approaching emotional experience. As a consequence, *The Glass Menagerie* is fundamentally a nonrealistic play. Distortion, illusion, dream, symbol, and myth are the tools by means of which the action onstage is endowed with beauty and meaning. A screen displays words and images relevant to the action; music intrudes with melodramatic timing; the lights rise or dim according to the mood onstage, not the time of day; symbols like the glass menagerie are hammered home in the dialogue without any attempt at subtlety. The play's style may best be described as expressionistic—underlying meaning is emphasized at the expense of realism. The play's lack of stylistic realism is further explained by the fact that the story is told from Tom's memory. As Tom puts it, the fact that what we are seeing is a memory play means that "it is dimly lighted, it is sentimental, it is not realistic. In memory everything seems to happen to music."

Though the style of the play is overwhelmingly nonrealistic, its content is a different matter. Williams also claimed that inventive stylistic devices like those he favored must never lead a play to "escape its responsibility of dealing with reality." Emotions like Tom's boredom, Amanda's nostalgia, and Laura's terror are conveyed with all the vividness of reality. So are the sorrowful hostility between Tom and Amanda and the quiet love between Tom and Laura. Similarly, the bleak lower-middle-class life of the Wingfield family is portrayed with a great deal of fidelity to historical and social realities. In fact, it often seems as if the main effect of the play's nonrealistic style is to increase the sense of reality surrounding its content. The play, as Tom says, is committed to giving its audience "truth in the pleasant disguise of illusion."

How to Write
Literary Analysis

The Literary Essay: A Step-by-Step Guide

When you read for pleasure, your only goal is enjoyment. You might find yourself reading to get caught up in an exciting story, to learn about an interesting time or place, or just to pass time. Maybe you're looking for inspiration, guidance, or a reflection of your own life. There are as many different, valid ways of reading a book as there are books in the world.

When you read a work of literature in an English class, however, you're being asked to read in a special way: you're being asked to perform *literary analysis*. To analyze something means to break it down into smaller parts and then examine how those parts work, both individually and together. Literary analysis involves examining all the parts of a novel, play, short story, or poem—elements such as character, setting, tone, and imagery—and thinking about how the author uses those elements to create certain effects.

A literary essay isn't a book review: you're not being asked whether or not you liked a book or whether you'd recommend it to another reader. A literary essay also isn't like the kind of book report you wrote when you were younger, where your teacher wanted you to summarize the book's action. A high school- or college-level literary essay asks, "How does this piece of literature actually work?" "How does it do what it does?" and, "Why might the author have made the choices he or she did?"

The Seven Steps
No one is born knowing how to analyze literature; it's a skill you learn and a process you can master. As you gain more practice with this kind of thinking and writing, you'll be able to craft a method that works best for you. But until then, here are seven basic steps to writing a well-constructed literary essay:

> *1. Ask questions*
> *2. Collect evidence*
> *3. Construct a thesis*

4. *Develop and organize arguments*
5. *Write the introduction*
6. *Write the body paragraphs*
7. *Write the conclusion*

---

1. ASK QUESTIONS

When you're assigned a literary essay in class, your teacher will often provide you with a list of writing prompts. Lucky you! Now all you have to do is choose one. Do yourself a favor and pick a topic that interests you. You'll have a much better (not to mention easier) time if you start off with something you enjoy thinking about. If you are asked to come up with a topic by yourself, though, you might start to feel a little panicked. Maybe you have too many ideas—or none at all. Don't worry. Take a deep breath and start by asking yourself these questions:

- **What struck you?** Did a particular image, line, or scene linger in your mind for a long time? If it fascinated you, chances are you can draw on it to write a fascinating essay.

- **What confused you?** Maybe you were surprised to see a character act in a certain way, or maybe you didn't understand why the book ended the way it did. Confusing moments in a work of literature are like a loose thread in a sweater: if you pull on it, you can unravel the entire thing. Ask yourself why the author chose to write about that character or scene the way he or she did and you might tap into some important insights about the work as a whole.

- **Did you notice any patterns?** Is there a phrase that the main character uses constantly or an image that repeats throughout the book? If you can figure out how that pattern weaves through the work and what the significance of that pattern is, you've almost got your entire essay mapped out.

- **Did you notice any contradictions or ironies?** Great works of literature are complex; great literary essays recognize and explain those complexities. Maybe the title (*Happy Days*) totally disagrees with the book's subject matter (hungry orphans dying in the woods). Maybe the main character acts one way around his family and a completely different way around his friends and associates. If you can find a way to explain a work's contradictory elements, you've got the seeds of a great essay.

At this point, you don't need to know exactly what you're going to say about your topic; you just need a place to begin your exploration. You can help direct your reading and brainstorming by formulating your topic as a *question,* which you'll then try to answer in your essay. The best questions invite critical debates and discussions, not just a rehashing of the summary. Remember, you're looking for something you can *prove or argue* based on evidence you find in the text. Finally, remember to keep the scope of your question in mind: is this a topic you can adequately address within the word or page limit you've been given? Conversely, is this a topic big enough to fill the required length?

GOOD QUESTIONS

"Are Romeo and Juliet's parents responsible for the deaths of their children?"

"Why do pigs keep showing up in LORD OF THE FLIES*?"*

"Are Dr. Frankenstein and his monster alike? How?"

BAD QUESTIONS

"What happens to Scout in TO KILL A MOCKINGBIRD*?"*

"What do the other characters in JULIUS CAESAR *think about Caesar?"*

"How does Hester Prynne in THE SCARLET LETTER *remind me of my sister?"*

---

2. COLLECT EVIDENCE

Once you know what question you want to answer, it's time to scour the book for things that will help you answer the question. Don't worry if you don't know what you want to say yet—right now you're just collecting ideas and material and letting it all percolate. Keep track of passages, symbols, images, or scenes that deal with your topic. Eventually, you'll start making connections between these examples and your thesis will emerge.

Here's a brief summary of the various parts that compose each and every work of literature. These are the elements that you will analyze in your essay, and which you will offer as evidence to support your arguments. For more on the parts of literary works, see the Glossary of Literary Terms at the end of this section.

ELEMENTS OF STORY   These are the *what*s of the work—what happens, where it happens, and to whom it happens.

- **Plot:** All of the events and actions of the work.

- **Character:** The people who act and are acted upon in a literary work. The main character of a work is known as the *protagonist*.

- **Conflict:** The central tension in the work. In most cases, the protagonist wants something, while opposing forces (antagonists) hinder the protagonist's progress.

- **Setting:** When and where the work takes place. Elements of setting include location, time period, time of day, weather, social atmosphere, and economic conditions.

- **Narrator:** The person telling the story. The narrator may straightforwardly report what happens, convey the subjective opinions and perceptions of one or more characters, or provide commentary and opinion in his or her own voice.

- **Themes:** The main idea or message of the work—usually an abstract idea about people, society, or life in general. A work may have many themes, which may be in tension with one another.

ELEMENTS OF STYLE   These are the *how*s—how the characters speak, how the story is constructed, and how language is used throughout the work.

- **Structure and organization:** How the parts of the work are assembled. Some novels are narrated in a linear, chronological fashion, while others skip around in time. Some plays follow a traditional three- or five-act structure, while others are a series of loosely connected scenes. Some authors deliberately leave gaps in their works, leaving readers to puzzle out the missing information. A work's structure and organization can tell you a lot about the kind of message it wants to convey.

- **Point of view:** The perspective from which a story is told. In *first-person point of view,* the narrator involves him or herself in the story. ("I went to the store"; "We watched in horror as the bird slammed into the window.") A first-person narrator is usually the protagonist of the work, but not always. In *third-person point of view,* the narrator does not participate in the story. A third-person narrator may closely follow a specific character, recounting that individual character's thoughts or experiences, or it may be what we call an *omniscient* narrator. Omniscient narrators see and know all: they can witness any event in any time or place and are privy to the inner thoughts and feelings of all characters. Remember that the narrator and the author are not the same thing!

- **Diction:** Word choice. Whether a character uses dry, clinical language or flowery prose with lots of exclamation points can tell you a lot about his or her attitude and personality.

- **Syntax:** Word order and sentence construction. Syntax is a crucial part of establishing an author's narrative voice. Ernest Hemingway, for example, is known for writing in very short, straightforward sentences, while James Joyce characteristically wrote in long, incredibly complicated lines.

- **Tone:** The mood or feeling of the text. Diction and syntax often contribute to the tone of a work. A novel written in short, clipped sentences that use small, simple words might feel brusque, cold, or matter-of-fact.

- **Imagery:** Language that appeals to the senses, representing things that can be seen, smelled, heard, tasted, or touched.

- **Figurative language:** Language that is not meant to be interpreted literally. The most common types of figurative language are *metaphors* and *similes,* which compare two unlike things in order to suggest a similarity between them— for example, "All the world's a stage," or "The moon is like a ball of green cheese." (Metaphors say one thing *is* another thing; similes claim that one thing is *like* another thing.)

---

3. CONSTRUCT A THESIS

When you've examined all the evidence you've collected and know how you want to answer the question, it's time to write your thesis statement. A *thesis* is a claim about a work of literature that needs to be supported by evidence and arguments. The thesis statement is the heart of the literary essay, and the bulk of your paper will be spent trying to prove this claim. A good thesis will be:

- **Arguable.** "*The Great Gatsby* describes New York society in the 1920s" isn't a thesis—it's a fact.

- **Provable through textual evidence**. "*Hamlet* is a confusing but ultimately very well-written play" is a weak thesis because it offers the writer's personal opinion about the book. Yes, it's arguable, but it's not a claim that can be proved or supported with examples taken from the play itself.

- **Surprising**. "Both George and Lenny change a great deal in *Of Mice and Men*" is a weak thesis because it's obvious. A really strong thesis will argue for a reading of the text that is not immediately apparent.

- **Specific**. "Dr. Frankenstein's monster tells us a lot about the human condition" is *almost* a really great thesis statement, but it's still too vague. What does the writer mean by "a lot"? *How* does the monster tell us so much about the human condition?

GOOD THESIS STATEMENTS

Question: In *Romeo and Juliet*, which is more powerful in shaping the lovers' story: fate or foolishness?

Thesis: "Though Shakespeare defines Romeo and Juliet as 'star-crossed lovers' and images of stars and planets appear throughout the play, a closer examination of that celestial imagery reveals that the stars are merely witnesses to the characters' foolish activities and not the causes themselves."

Question: How does the bell jar function as a symbol in Sylvia Plath's *The Bell Jar*?

Thesis: "A bell jar is a bell-shaped glass that has three basic uses: to hold a specimen for observation, to contain gases, and to maintain a vacuum. The bell jar appears in each of these capacities in *The Bell Jar*, Plath's semi-autobiographical novel, and each appearance marks a different stage in Esther's mental breakdown."

Question: Would Piggy in *The Lord of the Flies* make a good island leader if he were given the chance?

Thesis: "Though the intelligent, rational, and innovative Piggy has the mental characteristics of a good leader, he ultimately lacks the social skills necessary to be an effective one. Golding emphasizes this point by giving Piggy a foil in the charismatic Jack, whose magnetic personality allows him to capture and wield power effectively, if not always wisely."

4. DEVELOP AND ORGANIZE ARGUMENTS

The reasons and examples that support your thesis will form the middle paragraphs of your essay. Since you can't really write your thesis statement until you know how you'll structure your argument, you'll probably end up working on steps 3 and 4 at the same time.

There's no single method of argumentation that will work in every context. One essay prompt might ask you to compare and contrast two characters, while another asks you to trace an image through a given work of literature. These questions require different kinds of answers and therefore different kinds of arguments. Below, we'll discuss three common kinds of essay prompts and some strategies for constructing a solid, well-argued case.

TYPES OF LITERARY ESSAYS

- **Compare and contrast**

    *Compare and contrast the characters of Huck and Jim
    in* THE ADVENTURES OF HUCKLEBERRY FINN.

    Chances are you've written this kind of essay before. In an academic literary context, you'll organize your arguments the same way you would in any other class. You can either go *subject by subject* or *point by point*. In the former, you'll discuss one character first and then the second. In the latter, you'll choose several traits (attitude toward life, social status, images and metaphors associated with the character) and devote a paragraph to each. You may want to use a mix of these two approaches—for example, you may want to spend a paragraph a piece broadly sketching Huck's and Jim's personalities before transitioning into a paragraph or two that describes a few key points of comparison. This can be a highly effective strategy if you want to make a counterintuitive argument—that, despite seeming to be totally different, the two objects being compared are actually similar in a very important way (or vice versa). Remember that your essay should reveal something fresh or unexpected about the text, so think beyond the obvious parallels and differences.

- **Trace**

    *Choose an image—for example, birds, knives, or
    eyes—and trace that image throughout* MACBETH.

    Sounds pretty easy, right? All you need to do is read the play, underline every appearance of a knife in *Macbeth*, and then list them in your essay in the order they appear, right? Well, not exactly. Your teacher doesn't want a simple catalog of examples. He or she wants to see you make *connections* between those examples—that's the difference between summarizing and analyzing. In the *Macbeth* example above, think about the different contexts in which knives appear in the play and to what effect. In *Macbeth,* there are real knives and imagined knives; knives that kill and knives that simply threaten. Categorize and classify your examples to give them some order. Finally, always keep the overall effect in mind. After you choose and analyze your examples, you should come to some greater understanding about the work, as well as your chosen image, symbol, or phrase's role in developing the major themes and stylistic strategies of that work.

- **Debate**

  Is the society depicted in 1984 good for its citizens?

  In this kind of essay, you're being asked to debate a moral, ethical, or aesthetic issue regarding the work. You might be asked to judge a character or group of characters (*Is Caesar responsible for his own demise?*) or the work itself (*Is* JANE EYRE *a feminist novel?*). For this kind of essay, there are two important points to keep in mind. First, don't simply base your arguments on your personal feelings and reactions. Every literary essay expects you to read and analyze the work, so search for evidence in the text. What do characters in *1984* have to say about the government of Oceania? What images does Orwell use that might give you a hint about his attitude toward the government? As in any debate, you also need to make sure that you define all the necessary terms before you begin to argue your case. What does it mean to be a "good" society? What makes a novel "feminist"? You should define your terms right up front, in the first paragraph after your introduction.

  Second, remember that strong literary essays make contrary and surprising arguments. Try to think outside the box. In the *1984* example above, it seems like the obvious answer would be no, the totalitarian society depicted in Orwell's novel is *not* good for its citizens. But can you think of any arguments for the opposite side? Even if your final assertion is that the novel depicts a cruel, repressive, and therefore harmful society, acknowledging and responding to the counterargument will strengthen your overall case.

5. WRITE THE INTRODUCTION

Your introduction sets up the entire essay. It's where you present your topic and articulate the particular issues and questions you'll be addressing. It's also where you, as the writer, introduce yourself to your readers. A persuasive literary essay immediately establishes its writer as a knowledgeable, authoritative figure.

An introduction can vary in length depending on the overall length of the essay, but in a traditional five-paragraph essay it should be no longer than one paragraph. However long it is, your introduction needs to:

- **Provide any necessary context.** Your introduction should situate the reader and let him or her know what to expect. What book are you discussing? Which characters? What topic will you be addressing?

- **Answer the "So what?" question.** Why is this topic important, and why is your particular position on the topic noteworthy? Ideally, your introduction should pique the reader's interest by suggesting how your argument is surprising or otherwise counterintuitive. Literary essays make unexpected connections and reveal less-than-obvious truths.

- **Present your thesis.** This usually happens at or very near the end of your introduction.

- **Indicate the shape of the essay to come.** Your reader should finish reading your introduction with a good sense of the scope of your essay as well as the path you'll take toward proving your thesis. You don't need to spell out every step, but you do need to suggest the organizational pattern you'll be using.

Your introduction should not:

- **Be vague.** Beware of the two killer words in literary analysis: *interesting* and *important*. Of course the work, question, or example is interesting and important—that's why you're writing about it!

- **Open with any grandiose assertions.** Many student readers think that beginning their essays with a flamboyant statement such as, "Since the dawn of time, writers have been fascinated with the topic of free will," makes them sound important and commanding. You know what? It actually sounds pretty amateurish.

- **Wildly praise the work.** Another typical mistake student writers make is extolling the work or author. Your teacher doesn't need to be told that "Shakespeare is perhaps the greatest writer in the English language." You can mention a work's reputation in passing—by referring to *The Adventures of Huckleberry Finn* as "Mark Twain's enduring classic," for example—but don't make a point of bringing it up unless that reputation is key to your argument.

- **Go off-topic.** Keep your introduction streamlined and to the point. Don't feel the need to throw in all kinds of bells and whistles in order to impress your reader—just get to the point as quickly as you can, without skimping on any of the required steps.

---

6. Write the Body Paragraphs

Once you've written your introduction, you'll take the arguments you developed in step 4 and turn them into your body paragraphs. The organization of this middle section of your essay will largely be determined by the argumentative strategy you use, but no matter how you arrange your thoughts, your body paragraphs need to do the following:

- **Begin with a strong topic sentence.** Topic sentences are like signs on a highway: they tell the reader where they are and where they're going. A good topic sentence not only alerts readers to what issue will be discussed in the following paragraph but also gives them a sense of what argument will be made *about* that issue. "Rumor and gossip play an important role in *The Crucible*" isn't a strong topic sentence because it doesn't tell us very much. "The community's constant gossiping creates an environment that allows false accusations to flourish" is a much stronger topic sentence— it not only tells us *what* the paragraph will discuss (gossip) but *how* the paragraph will discuss the topic (by showing how gossip creates a set of conditions that leads to the play's climactic action).

- **Fully and completely develop a single thought.** Don't skip around in your paragraph or try to stuff in too much material. Body paragraphs are like bricks: each individual one needs to be strong and sturdy or the entire structure will collapse. Make sure you have really proven your point before moving on to the next one.

- **Use transitions effectively.** Good literary essay writers know that each paragraph must be clearly and strongly linked to the material around it. Think of each paragraph as a response to the one that precedes it. Use transition words and phrases such as *however, similarly, on the contrary, therefore,* and *furthermore* to indicate what kind of response you're making.

---

7. WRITE THE CONCLUSION

Just as you used the introduction to ground your readers in the topic before providing your thesis, you'll use the conclusion to quickly summarize the specifics learned thus far and then hint at the broader implications of your topic. A good conclusion will:

- **Do more than simply restate the thesis.** If your thesis argued that *The Catcher in the Rye* can be read as a Christian allegory, don't simply end your essay by saying, "And that is why *The Catcher in the Rye* can be read as a Christian allegory." If you've constructed your arguments well, this kind of statement will just be redundant.

- **Synthesize the arguments, not summarize them.** Similarly, don't repeat the details of your body paragraphs in your conclusion. The reader has already read your essay, and chances are it's not so long that they've forgotten all your points by now.

- **Revisit the "So what?" question.** In your introduction, you made a case for why your topic and position are important. You should close your essay with the same sort of gesture. What do your readers know now that they didn't know before? How will that knowledge help them better appreciate or understand the work overall?

- **Move from the specific to the general.** Your essay has most likely treated a very specific element of the work—a single character, a small set of images, or a particular passage. In your conclusion, try to show how this narrow discussion has wider implications for the work overall. If your essay on *To Kill a Mockingbird* focused on the character of Boo Radley, for example, you might want to include a bit in your

conclusion about how he fits into the novel's larger message
about childhood, innocence, or family life.

- **Stay relevant.** Your conclusion should suggest new directions
  of thought, but it shouldn't be treated as an opportunity to
  pad your essay with all the extra, interesting ideas you came
  up with during your brainstorming sessions but couldn't
  fit into the essay proper. Don't attempt to stuff in unrelated
  queries or too many abstract thoughts.

- **Avoid making overblown closing statements.** A conclusion
  should open up your highly specific, focused discussion, but
  it should do so without drawing a sweeping lesson about
  life or human nature. Making such observations may be
  part of the point of reading, but it's almost always a mistake
  in essays, where these observations tend to sound overly
  dramatic or simply silly.

A+ Essay Checklist

Congratulations! If you've followed all the steps we've outlined
above, you should have a solid literary essay to show for all your
efforts. What if you've got your sights set on an A+? To write the
kind of superlative essay that will be rewarded with a perfect grade,
keep the following rubric in mind. These are the qualities that teach-
ers expect to see in a truly A+ essay. How does yours stack up?

- ✓ Demonstrates a thorough understanding of the book
- ✓ Presents an original, compelling argument
- ✓ Thoughtfully analyzes the text's formal elements
- ✓ Uses appropriate and insightful examples
- ✓ Structures ideas in a logical and progressive order
- ✓ Demonstrates a mastery of sentence construction,
  transitions, grammar, spelling, and word choice

Suggested Essay Topics

1. *Who do you think is the main character of the play—Tom, Laura, or Amanda? Why? Is the main character the protagonist? Is there an antagonist?*

2. *What might happen to Laura after Tom's departure? What might happen to Amanda?*

3. *What is the effect of the images and phrases that appear on the screen throughout the play? Do they enhance or detract from the mood of what is occurring onstage?*

4. *Discuss the symbol of the glass menagerie. What does it represent? Does it represent the same things throughout the play, or does its meaning change?*

5. *Generally, plays do not have narrators. How does the fact that Tom is the narrator affect the style and content of the play? Would your appraisal of the events be different if there were no narrator?*

A+ STUDENT ESSAY

> Discuss the significance of the unicorn in *The Glass Menagerie*. How does the unicorn relate to the play's major themes?

In *The Glass Menagerie,* Laura Wingfield's unicorn represents a pure, unique soul that is damaged by contact with the world. Likewise, Laura herself radiates delicacy and purity, which she isn't able to retain fully after her dinner with the gentleman caller. In subtler ways, the play's three main characters lose some of their youthful hope and idealism to the constricting realities of adult life. The unicorn thus introduces Williams's theme of lost innocence, and it emphasizes his interest in the sacrifices his characters make as they grow older.

Williams emphasizes the uniqueness and purity of Laura's unicorn—qualities that are diminished when the outside world intrudes on the Wingfield dining room. Williams reminds us that the unicorn is glass, transparent, and completely unclouded. The unicorn's horn sets it apart from the other animals in the glass menagerie, because such a creature does not really exist in the world. Laura gives it special attention, emphasizing its distinction among its neighbors. When Jim, a representative of the outside world, visits for dinner, he remarks on the big, ungainly shadow he casts across the living room, begins a clumsy dance with Laura, knocks over the unicorn, and breaks its horn. Jim is the opposite of the unicorn—glass objects, after all, don't cast shadows—and his presence reduces the unicorn to a damaged, ordinary object. A unicorn without a horn is nothing more than a mundane horse. By contact with the world, the unicorn has lost some of its distinctiveness and purity.

Like the unicorn, Laura initially radiates uniqueness and innocence. Her high-school nickname, "Blue Roses," suggests not only delicacy but also otherworldliness: Blue roses, like unicorns, do not exist in the real world. Laura stays home all day to tend to her glass figures, but in reality her hobby provides her with an excuse to avoid real-world adult commitments, such as typing school and dating, that her mother tries to force on her. Like the unicorn, Laura loses some of her purity through contact with Jim. Having thought she could indulge a childhood fantasy and fall in love with Jim, she learns that he is already engaged and has merely been flirting with her. Laura now has an understanding of the way the world works: People do not always say what they mean, and men have a startling capacity to hurt her. Laura offers the unicorn to Jim as a "souvenir," suggesting that the unicorn and its wounds symbolize the pain she has experienced over dinner. Contact with Jim has stripped her of some of her childlike innocence, leaving her slightly more ordinary and damaged, like her unicorn.

The other three characters in *The Glass Menagerie* are not as fragile and childlike as Laura; however, each of them has also lost a precious, youthful hope in the draining struggle to survive adulthood. Jim recalls high-school dreams of glory in basketball and music, yet the economic realities of 1930s Missouri have reduced him to a factory worker who spouts clichés about the "inferiority complex," the importance of public speaking, and monogamous bliss with a "girl" he finds "just fine." Amanda longs to return to youthful days of courting and chivalry, and the peals of her girlish laughter that echo throughout the climactic scene make audible her struggle to return to the past. The husband who deserted her has crushed her dream of having a simple, romantic life. Tom yearns to write poetry and escape, but his helpless, needy family has forced him to take a factory job. (Williams brutally reminds us that, when he finally does decide to begin an artistic career, Tom must abandon his family and stop paying the light bills. As a result, the electric company shuts off the Wingfields' lights in the climactic scene.) In each case, exposure to the devastating economic and interpersonal realities of adult life reduces, saddens, and damages the characters in *The Glass Menagerie*.

Laura's unicorn thus symbolizes the painful transition each of Williams's four characters makes from a hopeful, confident childhood to a timid and deadening existence as an adult. The unicorn has a radiance, transparency, and rarity that Jim damages in his brief visit to the Wingfield house, just as he also damages Laura's own extraordinary innocence and fragility. Each of the characters has surrendered major dreams: Tom, his poetic ambition; Amanda, her belief in romance; Jim, his high-school talents. Williams uses the unicorn to quickly and unforgettably symbolize the devastation life has wrought on each of his tragic characters.

GLOSSARY OF LITERARY TERMS

ANTAGONIST

The entity that acts to frustrate the goals of the *protagonist*. The antagonist is usually another *character* but may also be a non-human force.

ANTIHERO / ANTIHEROINE

A *protagonist* who is not admirable or who challenges notions of what should be considered admirable.

CHARACTER

A person, animal, or any other thing with a personality that appears in a *narrative*.

CLIMAX

The moment of greatest intensity in a text or the major turning point in the *plot*.

CONFLICT

The central struggle that moves the *plot* forward. The conflict can be the *protagonist*'s struggle against fate, nature, society, or another person.

FIRST-PERSON POINT OF VIEW

A literary style in which the *narrator* tells the story from his or her own *point of view* and refers to himself or herself as "I." The narrator may be an active participant in the story or just an observer.

HERO / HEROINE

The principal *character* in a literary work or *narrative*.

IMAGERY

Language that brings to mind sense-impressions, representing things that can be seen, smelled, heard, tasted, or touched.

MOTIF

A recurring idea, structure, contrast, or device that develops or informs the major *themes* of a work of literature.

NARRATIVE

A story.

NARRATOR

The person (sometimes a *character*) who tells a story; the *voice* assumed by the writer. The narrator and the author of the work of literature are not the same person.

PLOT

The arrangement of the events in a story, including the sequence in which they are told, the relative emphasis they are given, and the causal connections between events.

POINT OF VIEW

The *perspective* that a *narrative* takes toward the events it describes.

PROTAGONIST

The main *character* around whom the story revolves.

SETTING

The location of a *narrative* in time and space. Setting creates mood or atmosphere.

SUBPLOT

A secondary *plot* that is of less importance to the overall story but may serve as a point of contrast or comparison to the main plot.

SYMBOL

An object, *character,* figure, or color that is used to represent an abstract idea or concept. Unlike an *emblem,* a symbol may have different meanings in different contexts.

SYNTAX

The way the words in a piece of writing are put together to form lines, phrases, or clauses; the basic structure of a piece of writing.

THEME

A fundamental and universal idea explored in a literary work.

TONE

The author's attitude toward the subject or *characters* of a story or poem or toward the reader.

VOICE

An author's individual way of using language to reflect his or her own personality and attitudes. An author communicates voice through *tone, diction,* and *syntax.*

A NOTE ON PLAGIARISM

Plagiarism—presenting someone else's work as your own—rears its ugly head in many forms. Many students know that copying text without citing it is unacceptable. But some don't realize that even if you're not quoting directly, but instead are paraphrasing or summarizing, *it is plagiarism* unless you cite the source.

Here are the most common forms of plagiarism:

- Using an author's phrases, sentences, or paragraphs without citing the source
- Paraphrasing an author's ideas without citing the source
- Passing off another student's work as your own

How do you steer clear of plagiarism? You should *always* acknowledge all words and ideas that aren't your own by using quotation marks around verbatim text or citations like footnotes and endnotes to note another writer's ideas. For more information on how to give credit when credit is due, ask your teacher for guidance or visit www.sparknotes.com.

REVIEW & RESOURCES

QUIZ

1. Where does Tom work?

    A. At a pharmacy
    B. At a shoe warehouse
    C. At a flower shop
    D. For a newspaper

2. What does Tom like to write?

    A. Poetry
    B. Musical librettos
    C. Journalistic dispatches
    D. Bad checks

3. Where does *The Glass Menagerie* take place?

    A. Cleveland
    B. New York City
    C. Mississippi
    D. St. Louis

4. At the beginning of the play, where is Laura supposedly attending classes?

    A. At a language school
    B. At a business college
    C. At a dance academy
    D. At a high school

5. *The Glass Menagerie* is a "memory play." From which character's memory is it drawn?

    A. Tom's
    B. Amanda's
    C. Laura's
    D. Mr. Wingfield's

6. For what does Amanda conduct a telephone campaign in order to make extra money?

   A. A local election
   B. Magazine subscriptions
   C. A charity
   D. Temperance

7. Amanda returns a library book that Tom has checked out. Who is the author of this book?

   A. Hart Crane
   B. Frederick Nietzsche
   C. Henrik Ibsen
   D. D. H. Lawrence

8. The action of the play is set nearest to which era of American history?

   A. Reconstruction
   B. The Great Depression
   C. The Roaring Twenties
   D. The Swell Fifties

9. According to Tom, where does he spend most of his nights?

   A. At smoky jazz joints
   B. At the movies
   C. At his best girl's house
   D. At the offices of the *Cleveland Plain Dealer*

10. What is Amanda most concerned that Tom's friend, the gentleman caller, not be?

    A. Overly intelligent
    B. Canadian
    C. A drunk
    D. Tubercular

11. In what is Jim taking night courses?

    A. Radio engineering and public speaking
    B. Home economics and desktop publishing
    C. Business administration and product development
    D. Sufi asceticism and Pure Land Buddhism

12. For whom did Tom's father work?

    A. A canned goods business
    B. The Department of the Interior
    C. A glue manufacturer
    D. The telephone company

13. What do the Wingfields have instead of a porch?

    A. A marble balcony
    B. A fire-escape landing
    C. The neighbor's roof
    D. Cable TV

14. What is Laura's favorite animal among her glass figurines?

    A. A fawn
    B. A leopard
    C. A dinosaur
    D. A unicorn

15. What is Jim's nickname for Tom?

    A. Marlowe
    B. Jonson
    C. Webster
    D. Shakespeare

16. What class did Jim and Laura have together in high school?

    A. Wood shop
    B. Chorus
    C. Spanish III
    D. Metal shop

17. Of what origin is Jim's family?

    A.   Irish
    B.   African-American
    C.   Spanish
    D.   Russian

18. Why did Jim call Laura "Blue Roses"?

    A.   Because she wore blue roses in her hair
    B.   Because it was the title of a popular song
    C.   Because it sounds like "pleurosis"
    D.   Because he called all the girls that

19. How does Tom plunge the family into darkness?

    A.   By not paying the water bill
    B.   By not paying the gas bill
    C.   By not paying the phone bill
    D.   By not paying the light bill

20. For what does Tom pay membership dues with the money earmarked for the abovementioned bill?

    A.   The Union of Industrial Shipping Clerks and Stockmen
    B.   The Union of Merchant Seamen
    C.   The United Brotherhood of Railcar Porters
    D.   The Society of Poets and Writers

21. What is across the alley from the Wingfields' apartment?

    A.   A church
    B.   A speakeasy
    C.   A library
    D.   A dance hall

22. Why will Jim not call again on the Wingfields?

    A.   He is too shy
    B.   He is engaged
    C.   He is leaving town
    D.   He is put off by Laura

23. What, according to Tom, is man by instinct?

   A.   A lover, a hunter, a fighter
   B.   A dancer, a singer, a cook
   C.   A sprinter, a builder, an achiever
   D.   A poet, a martyr, a soothsayer

24. What does Amanda make Tom promise that he will never be?

   A.   A lawyer
   B.   A drunkard
   C.   An oboist
   D.   A money lender

25. How did Tennessee Williams refer to the 1960s?

   A.   As his "everlasting summer of love"
   B.   As his "stoned age"
   C.   As "the winter of my discontent"
   D.   As "the age of revolution through theatre"

Suggestions for Further Reading

BLOOM, HAROLD, ed. *Tennessee Williams's* THE GLASS MENAGERIE (Bloom's Modern Critical Interpretations). New York: Chelsea House Publishers, 2007.

LONDRE, FELICIA HARDISON. *Tennessee Williams.* New York: Frederick Ungar Publishers, 1979.

LUMLEY, FREDERICK. *Trends in 20th Century Drama.* New York: Oxford University Press, 1960.

O'CONNOR, JACQUELINE. *Dramatizing Dementia: Madness in the Plays of Tennessee Williams.* Bowling Green, Ohio: Bowling Green State University Popular Press, 1997.

SIEBOLD, THOMAS, ed. *Readings on* THE GLASS MENAGERIE. San Diego: Greenhaven Press, 1998.

SPOTO, DONALD. *The Kindness of Strangers: The Life of Tennessee Williams.* New York: Da Capo Press, 1997.

WILLIAMS, TENNESSEE. *Memoirs (New Edition).* Garden City, New York: New Directions, 2006.

————. *Notebooks.* Margaret Bradham Thornton, ed. New Haven: Yale University Press, 2007.